Bev

Welcome to the [...]
And thanks for welcoming us & your
Your presentation was inspiring, light

IS EVERYONE AT THE TABLE?   for the table

Emi Tekio Talkwa
Tamés
Oct 6/ 2011
Sx Morgut,
Cammunde, fr Tucker

# IS EVERYONE AT THE TABLE?

## 18 LIFE LESSONS
## IN PROBLEM SOLVING

---

### A Note About the Cover Illustration

How do bouncing balls relate to ADR?

Small rubber balls proved to be an effective ice breaker for a group of youths during my opening remarks to a four-day conference on youth conflict resolution in Ottawa in 2007. Balls were thrown out to each of the 80 young participants from across Canada, producing laughter and an energetic discussion. To my pleasant surprise, later that week when the 40 adult chaperones arrived for my second keynote address, they asked for balls also! The balls created a connection between all the participants and demonstrated a symbolic ADR principle: even when we have differences, we can always find practical tools to help us interact—and we shouldn't forget to have fun too.

For more details on the bouncing balls story, please visit www.adrcentre.org.

To see the materials from the youth conflict resolution conference, please visit www.ethnocultural.ca.

# Is Everyone at the Table?

## 18 LIFE LESSONS IN PROBLEM SOLVING

Ernest G. Tannis

B.A., J.D., C. Med., Acc. FM (OAFM)

Solicitor, Mediator, Ontario Notary Public, Negotiation Consultant

Member of the Law Society of Upper Canada

Illustrated by Jim Turner

Published by the ADR Centre (Canada) Inc.

© Ernest G. Tannis
ISBN 978-0-9813864-1-6

Published by the ADR Centre (Canada) Inc.
Legal deposit 2010
Library and Archives Canada

Printed in Canada

Front cover: Photos.com
Back cover: Illustration by Jim Turner

**Library and Archives Canada Cataloguing in Publication**

Tannis, Ernest G., 1948-
Is everyone at the table? : 18 life lessons in problem solving / Ernest G. Tannis.

ISBN 978-0-9813864-1-6

1. Self-actualization (Psychology)--Case studies.  2. Problem solving--Case
studies.  3. Mediation--Case studies.  4. Interpersonal conflict--Prevention--
Case studies.  I. Title.

BF637.S4T35 2010        158.1        C2010-907371-1
KF9084.T35 2010

# DEDICATION

To my magnificent wife, Youmna Ismail; her parents, Hajj
Ahmad and Haji Fatima; her sisters, Shahrazad, Gina, Rabia,
and May; her brothers, Ossama and Moodie; and extended
family members, without whose loving support over the
years I would not have been able to complete this sequel
book, and who provided the gift of **A** **D**iscerning **R**estart
for my life. Thank you, shukran, merci beaucoup.

# CONTENTS

# ACKNOWLEDGEMENTS

It would literally take an entire book to properly recognize every person who has influenced my ADR journey, encouraged me or taught me lessons along the way. I wish to express my deep appreciation to several key individuals who have championed this book from the beginning and provided unwavering support throughout. Their contributions have taken many forms, and each one has been essential in ensuring this sequel book became a reality: Joellene Adams and many others from Akwesasne, Anastasia Bendus, Paul Bendus, Robert P. Birt, Beverley Britton, Charles (Skip) Brooks, Kerri Brooks-Richard, Dave Brown, Tom Colosi, Julie Desmarais, Brian Donald, Marie Francis, Marnie Francis, Paul Francis, Qais Ghanem, June Girvan, Gus Heidemann, Ben Hoffman, Richard Jackman, Emile Kanim, Lenny Lombardi, Melinda MacDonald, Shelagh Macdonald, Al MacMillan, Dan McCurdy, John W. McDonald, Christel McDonald, Michael McIntyre, Gary Michaels, George Millar, Ed Napke, Eli Nasrallah, Esper Nasrallah, Julien Payne, Phyllis Reading, Justin Richard, Gordon Shanks, Susan Shearouse, Victor Sheperd, Osman Siddiqui and family, Ron Suter, Chanda Tannis, Derek Tannis, Mike Tannis, Ralph Tannis, Janet Waitman, Harry Weldon, Vern White, and Jeremy Wright (1937–2009). And of course I must acknowledge all those who were involved in these stories, who had the courage, wisdom and stamina to explore other options to settle their differences. Thank you to all.

I would like to recognize and thank Esther van Gennip, my dear friend and colleague in ADR training and intervention, whose contributions helped form the basis for this book. Perhaps more than anyone else, Esther appreciated the potential of the stories, and she encouraged me to present them in a way that would be useful both for practitioners and the general public.

I have had the good fortune to be involved with a wide variety of civil societies, and charitable and social justice organizations, and these interactions have shaped my efforts in ADR. I would like to thank, in no deliberate order, the following organizations and their stakeholders for their care and attention to the well-being of our communities: Reach Canada, a charitable organization providing *pro bono* legal services and educational programs for persons with disabilities (www.reach.ca), the Canadian Institute for Conflict Resolution (www.cicr-icrc.ca), Canadian Council of the Blind (www.ccbnational.net), Leadership Ottawa (www.leadershipottawa.org), Universal Peace Federation (www.upf.org), National Capital Peace Council, Circle of Canadians, City of Peace Ottawa (www.mycityofpeace.com), Ontario Association for Family Mediation (www.oafm.on.ca) and particularly the Ottawa region chapter (www.familymediationottawa.com), The Collaborative Law Network (www.collaborativepracticeottawa.ca), Every Child Is Sacred, Dialogue With Diversity (www.dialoguewithdiversity.com), Institute for Multi-Track Diplomacy (www.imtd.org), the ADR Institute of Ontario (www.adrontario.ca), and The Man Kind Project (www.mankindproject.org).

I would like to pay tribute to two gentlemen who influenced my journey in countless ways and inspired me to complete this book. First, I would like to remember the Rt. Hon. Ramon Hnatyshyn (1934–2002), former Governor General of Canada, former Minister of Justice and Attorney General for Canada, and the second honorary chair of Reach Canada. By 2002 I had started to think in very general terms about eventually writing a second book, and I emailed him in July of that year with a request. On July 24 he so kindly replied to my email: "Ernie, thank you for this…Of course, I will be happy to write a foreword for your new book…" Sadly, he passed away later that year. I would also like to acknowledge the influence of Gordon Henderson (1912–1993), the first honorary chair of Reach Canada, who from the outset provided unqualified encouragement of my various efforts in the area of social justice. With his prescient backing of ADR with the Windsor-Essex Mediation Project (1981–1984) and his unflagging support, I gained the confidence to continue with this ADR journey, leading some to call these ADR efforts both "proleptic" and "iconoclastic." In 1988 his recommendation to the County of Carleton Law Association that I speak about ADR at their prestigious annual litigation conference eventually led to the unexpected publication of that paper as my first book,

*ADR That Works!*, for which Mr. Henderson wrote the foreword. I am grateful to both these gentlemen for their mentorship. May their memories be eternal.

I am indebted to the publishing team, whose skills and encouragement throughout brought this book to life and shelf. Robbi Hay facilitated the project to a point where it could be completed by the team, and her vision and nudging for these ADR books provided the basis for their emergence. Designer Miriam Bloom of Expression Communications Inc., has given unfailing support throughout, and her design skills, along with those of Donna Bates, resulted in a magnificent production. Illustrator Jim Turner has contributed not only imaginative drawings but also overall support at so many levels to ensure that the book came alive.

Finally, I would like to thank my editor, Brenda Quinn, who had an enormous task. She said to me at the beginning of this process, "Ernie, my job is to make sure your words don't get in the way of your meaning." She invested countless hours in research and editing to make the stories come to life, and was a valued consultant on every aspect. The editing of the stories was itself a give-and-take negotiation! Without her dedication and careful attention, this book would never have been completed. With my earnest thanks, Brenda.

*E.G.T.*

# HOW THIS BOOK CAME TO BE

Since 1998 Ernie and I have worked closely in delivering mediation training at all levels and together have conducted many interventions. Often when I have facilitated workshops I have invited Ernie to share his experiences with participants. Each time, people have expressed how much they learned through his stories and original quotes, and commented that they should be recorded in a book. That said, we began this journey of compiling his teachings.

Ernie is a pioneer and visionary leader in the field of ADR. He has been involved in many high-profile interventions, yet he shares his experiences as an ADR practitioner with humility and an attitude of gratitude. From the trials and tribulations of interventions he has conducted over the years he offers insights into teachings that guide individuals through times of chaos into clarity. This book not only reflects the journey of a man who seeks social justice for all, but also offers lessons in problem solving, and insights into principles and practices that foster "**A D**ignified **R**esolution."

Throughout this collection of real-life mediation stories Ernie weaves the stages of an ADR process:

*Preparation:*
The process begins by building trust and convening parties in conflict to apply problem-solving processes.

*Story:*
The ADR practitioner "hears the story" and creates a safe space for people to speak their truth.

*Interests, beliefs and value:*
The mediator invites parties in conflict to identify key issues, and reflect on values and principles that influence how they handle conflict.

*Options and choices:*
The process explores the "common ground" and encourages parties to consider options and choices to resolve their conflict.

*Objective criteria:*
With the best alternatives to a negotiated agreement (BATNA) laid on the table, disputants measure viable and realistic outcomes.

*Mutually acceptable agreement:*
Finally, the process supports the parties in moving towards a mutually beneficial solution.

It was an honour and privilege for me to work with Ernie in capturing these experiences in a manner that mirrors the stages of the ADR process. Each chapter provides valuable lessons for those interested in creative problem solving and the field of ADR.

This book is a practical resource guide and tool for mediators, facilitators, negotiators, managers, community leaders, students, teachers, parents, decision makers, professional advisors—and anyone interested in gaining a deeper understanding of ADR principles that work.

*Esther van Gennip*
Chartered Mediator, ADR Institute of Canada
Honoured Fellow, CICR
www.adrpractitioner.com

# FOREWORD

Ernie Tannis is the nineteenth "universal principle" of alternative dispute resolution (ADR) at work!

He has dedicated over 30 years of his legal career to this issue, and is one of the pioneers of Canada's movement in this field.

I remember in the 1980s when Ernie decided to provide options to clients, in addition to court, because he wanted them to be aware of the full spectrum of ADR processes available for problem solving. Some thought he was crazy to do this. However, he was just ahead of his time. Many years later, with the visionary support of leading members of the judiciary, the bar, and the ministry of the attorney general, the Ontario Superior Court of Justice in the city of Ottawa required that all civil suits had to go through a mandatory court-annexed mediation process before the case could proceed any further.

For five years Ernie conceived, organized, managed, and hosted a one-hour radio talk show on ADR. This incredible outreach to the public proved to be a force in educating citizens in their understanding of the benefits of ADR. This radio program was unequaled in the world.

The 18 universal principles in this book are really 18 stories based on Ernie's own career experiences. After each story he adds "some lessons" to be learned and draws conclusions from the stories that are easy to understand.

This is a remarkable, highly readable, and insightful collection of real-world events that prove the importance of ADR's ability to resolve conflicts, peacefully, in today's world.

*John W. McDonald, U.S. Ambassador (ret.)*
Chairman and CEO, Institute for Multi-Track Diplomacy
(www.imtd.org), Arlington, Virginia

Author of *The Shifting Grounds of Conflict and Peacebuilding: Stories and Lessons* (Lexington Books, 2008)

# PREFACE

*We must move from law and order to love and order.*

Completing this book has been a cathartic experience and I very much appreciate the nudging from those who cared enough to ensure it was completed. Selecting 18 chapters from 18,000 options has been a challenge! This became part of my own continuing healing process, as each life is indeed "a work in progress."

In seeking to find a proper preface for this sequel book, I felt a reflection of what has happened in my own life might help readers better appreciate how and why I personally can relate to each person's struggles, trials and tribulations, and why I believe that problem solving is needed by every human being every day in every type of relationship and situation.

It's well known that our childhood years have a permanent impact on our entire lives, consciously or unconsciously. My earliest memory is from age five, when I witnessed violence against someone who was protecting me. Over the years, I came to comprehend how that childhood trauma may have been a foundation for my relentless reaching out to help others in need, especially the vulnerable sectors of our society, to make up for that little boy who could not help the person protecting him. Social justice has been a central theme of my career and life since the beginning of my law practice.

Our mother raised four children on her own (me, my older sister and two older brothers), our father having left the house when I was about five years old. My father, from Lebanon, was a self-educated and innovative businessman who loved books. I was just beginning law school when he passed away around age 60, and I saw how estate issues require considerable conflict resolution over time. For many years I assisted my mother through the painful experience of dealing with and seeking to protect her rights against my father's estate. Again, I learned firsthand how disputes come very close to home and people need skills in communication and problem solving throughout their lives.

I could not have known then how necessary these problem-solving skills would be in the life transitions that were yet to come. I have been divorced and widowed, and through both their hardships and their blessings I have had to learn about maintaining respectful relationships. As a result of all this, I have been emboldened to the true value of these ADR principles as I have had to apply them in my own life.

Before my wife Mary passed away, she told me that if anything happened to her I was to do five things. I remember asking her, "Why are you talking like that?" She did not answer but asked me to pay attention. That week, she had a fatal heart attack at work, in the early morning. I often say now that everyone should be careful what they say to their loved ones, since every communication could be their last. These lessons and her final loving comments are ingrained in my heart.

One of her instructions was that I should get married again, and to a woman from my father's homeland, Lebanon. As it turned out, I married Youmna Ismail, who had been my client years before when I acted *pro bono* on her behalf to help her collect the *mahr,* a document signed at an Islamic marriage ceremony in which the husband promises to pay money or provide assets upon a divorce. She did finally collect after court-annexed mediation, which created a kind of social precedent at that time. The Canadian Bar Association recognized Ottawa as the first city in Canada to have court-annexed mediation and, having supported that initiative originally, I was especially pleased to have this case settled this way. In fact, at least 40 percent of court files are resolved as a result of this intervention process early on.

Some years after Youmna's case was settled I was living alone as a widower and a Muslim man I met quite by chance said I looked lonely. He told me that in his culture people believed in moving on and added that he had already recommended me to the sister of someone he knew. The sister, of course, turned out to be Youmna, and unbeknownst to him I already knew her and her family. What a coincidence. Life again had presented one problem and led me to a solution from unexpected sources.

On one occasion I took Youmna and her family to visit my mother, who at that time had dementia. My mother did not know Youmna or her family, or even recognize who she was speaking with most of the time, but she pointed to Youmna and told her to take care of me! At our wedding, Youmna's sister Rabia said that even a mother who has no memory knows in her heart what is good for her son. Again, one needs to pay attention to signs in life. In yet another coincidence, Youmna was born in a village in Lebanon just half an hour from my father's village. (I was born in Ottawa, however.) I was thus able to fulfill Mary's instruction, and in fact have since fulfilled all five of her instructions.

Since 1981 every facet of my professional and personal life has encompassed ADR. I always joke that this was all designed so that I can get along better with those around me, and if anyone else benefits, that is a bonus! I often think about all the mistakes I made along the way, but I have few regrets. There have been many dark times, but I believe

it would have been a grave mistake not to have pursued this course. I have been so fulfilled (and sometimes frustrated, too!) to have had so many challenges and opportunities, and I am grateful to be able to share them in the form of these stories. Isn't that how we learn from and lean on each other, by telling our stories?

All of this brings up how we find solutions in life in any circumstance. Every culture has its own ancient teachings about problem solving, and as an example I would like to share a famous story known as the 18th camel story:

A tribal leader left his herd of camels to his three sons. The herd was to be divided among the sons as follows: one half was to go to the eldest son, one third to the middle son, and one ninth to the youngest. The problem was that the herd had only 17 camels, so the sons began to quarrel viciously. (Imagine that—another quarrel over an estate!) At someone's suggestion they brought in a mediator from another village. After hearing the story, this person promised to reflect on the situation and return the next day.

The next day the mediator returned to the tribe, bringing a camel to add to the herd, and told the three sons they could now divide up the herd of 18 camels. So the eldest son took his half, which is 9; the middle son took his third, which is 6; and the youngest son took his ninth, which is 2, for a total of 17 camels. Thus the person who gave them the 18th camel was able to take it back!

This story never ceases to amaze people, and for many years I have been researching its origins. According to websites that study mathematical metaphors from different cultures, it is generally thought to be of Arabic or Hindu origin but none of them can cite any definitive source. My latest search led me to www.nasrudin-stories.com, which states that the teaching is from Imam Ali, revered in the Shia Muslim community as their founder. More research may uncover other sources.

There are many other examples of these problem-solving principles; in my Lebanese ancestry, the word *sulha* means reconciliation. Archbishop Desmond Tutu explained the African concept of *ubuntu* as follows: "It is about the essence of being human...It embraces hospitality, caring about others, being able to go the extra mile for the sake of others..."[1] These universal metaphors, these overreaching principles, can be found in the teachings and traditions of most cultures.

All this has brought me full circle to this sequel book, drawing on my own life background. With deference to all those who have guided this ADR path and to those whose stories are related here (with confidentialities protected), and thanks to all the support I have received, I have finally been able to finish this book.

I would like to end this preface with a quote from Mahatma Gandhi's autobiography. I trust this will provide a bridge as we continue to travel together along this ADR journey.

*"I hope and pray that no one will regard the advice interspersed in these chapters as authoritative. The experiments narrated should be regarded as illustrations, in light of which all people may carry on their own experiments according to their own inclinations and capacity."*[2]

*Ernest G. Tannis*
Ottawa, Ontario, Canada
November 2010
info@adrcentre.org
www.adrcentre.org

---

1  Quote from http://www.tutufoundationuk.org/ubuntu.html. Accessed November 1, 2010.
2  Mohandas K. Gandhi, *An Autobiography: The Story of My Experiments with Truth,* translated by Mahadev Desai (1927; reprint, Boston: Beacon Press, 1993).

# IS EVERYONE AT THE TABLE?

## 18 LIFE LESSONS
## IN PROBLEM SOLVING

# 1 IS EVERYONE AT THE TABLE?

*When the world is no longer under your feet, all you have left to stand on is what you stood for.*

IN 1989, THE PEOPLE of the Mohawk territory of Kanesatake were outraged to learn that the neighbouring town of Oka, Quebec planned to expand a golf course onto land the Mohawks considered their sacred burial ground. After trying for a year to stop the golf course expansion through the courts, in the spring of 1990 the Mohawks barricaded the land to block access.

In late April 1990, as the nation waited for the next chapter at Oka to unfold, 90 minutes away in the Mohawk territory of Akwesasne the long-simmering internal strife had boiled over, touched off by a gaming licence on the American side of the territory.

> A very important symbol is the empty chair at the negotiating table.

Akwesasne had always been very complex politically, divided by the Canada-U.S. border, split into numerous different factions, and governed by three separate bodies: the elected Mohawk Council for Akwesasne (MCA) on the Canadian side, an elected tribal council on the U.S. side, and the self-governing traditional Longhouse chiefs.

During five days of violence that some likened to a civil war two young Mohawk men were killed. In the midst of the fighting, the Canadian side of Akwesasne was evacuated to Cornwall, Ontario, and approximately 900 police officers from many jurisdictions descended on Akwesasne to attempt to restore order.

Following the evacuation, a friend who was the legal counsel for the MCA on the Canadian side invited me to Cornwall to meet with the grand chief and other leaders in an attempt to mediate a solution.

One of the alternative dispute resolution (ADR) principles I had learned at the time was the importance of continually asking, "Is everyone at the table?" and ensuring that every stakeholder is involved in the mediation process. A

very important symbol of this principle is the empty chair at the negotiating table. The empty chair is held for those who are already involved in the negotiating process and cannot be there at that time, or for those who have not yet arrived. If the chair is ever filled, another empty chair should always take its place, and throughout the negotiation the question must continue to be asked, "Who else should be at the table?"

But that was not the kind of negotiating process that the Mohawk leadership had envisioned. My colleagues and I had begun our work in the territory with an initial two-week listening exercise and, following the release of our report recommending the establishment of a mediation centre, the next stage was to talk to all the factions in the territory. I intended to open up the process to everyone and allow everyone's voice to be heard. The Mohawk leaders, however, said they would determine whom I could talk to, and insisted that one faction be excluded because of their suspected paramilitary associations. This faction was known as the Warrior Society but the Mohawk name, *Rotisken'rakéhte*, meant "the guardians and protectors of the community."

I emphasized again to the Mohawk leaders that my intent from the very beginning had always been to invite every stakeholder to the negotiating table, but they were adamant in their opposition. After an impasse of several days I went back to my friend, the legal counsel.

"It's a great honour to be involved in this," I said, "but unless I am allowed to talk to every party, in good conscience I cannot continue with the negotiation and will have to withdraw." After a few days we were finally given unrestricted access to everyone.

As negotiations began in Akwesasne to resolve long-standing conflicts, tensions were still mounting in Kanesatake as the Mohawks continued to barricade the land to stop the Oka golf course expansion. In July 1990, after the Mohawks had ignored several court injunctions ordering the removal of the barricades, Oka's mayor asked the Quebec provincial police, Sûreté du Québec (SQ), to intervene because of concerns over criminal activity around the barricade.

On July 11, 1990 a SWAT team stormed the Mohawk barricade and the confrontation turned violent. It is not clear which side opened fire first, but in the short gun battle that followed SQ Corporal Marcel Lemay was killed. The SQ backed off, leaving behind police cruisers and erecting its own barricade to restrict access to Kanesatake. It was the beginning of the Oka Crisis, a 78-day armed standoff that gained international attention.

In the days that followed, the situation intensified on both sides of the barricades. The Mohawks at Kanesatake were joined by Native people from across Canada and the U.S., including many from the Warrior Society in Akwesasne. The nearby Mohawk territory of Kahnawake showed its support by barricading a bridge and several highways leading into Montreal, creating enormous traffic problems and angering commuters. For its part, the SQ received reinforcements from the RCMP and then from Canadian Forces troops.

**I intended to allow everyone's voice to be heard.**

Against this backdrop of increasing tensions in Kanesatake, just 90 minutes away in Akwesasne my colleagues and I continued to meet with the various groups as part of the process of developing the mediation centre. Among those we met were people associated with the Warrior Society, but we were well aware that most of their members and leaders were involved in the Oka Crisis. We learned later that those we met with were passing along information to the Warrior Society leadership at Oka, allowing them to keep tabs on the situation in Akwesasne.

On September 26, 1990 the Oka Crisis finally ended. The Mohawks dismantled their weapons, threw them in a fire and walked back to the reserve, although many were

arrested by the SQ. The Government of Canada later bought the disputed land and cancelled the golf course expansion.

I finally met the self-proclaimed war chief of the Warrior Society when he returned to Akwesasne from Oka. I was surprised to discover he already knew of me and had checked me out. He said he knew I was well intentioned but nonetheless he was very suspicious of the mediation process since he had once been betrayed.

"Why have you taken so long to involve the Warrior Society?" he asked, adding that he knew I'd been talking to other groups in Akwesasne.

"My intention has always been to have every stakeholder at the table," I said, and showed him all the communication that had been exchanged, all of it documenting my goal of including everyone in the process. I added that I had threatened to leave the negotiations if that condition was not met. All this evidence apparently convinced the war chief, and I spent the next several weeks meeting with the Warrior Society members.

As a result of the mediation exercise the Mohawks in Akwesasne did eventually create a mediation centre, which helped them resolve their internal strife and their continuing conflicts with government and police.

Several months after the Oka Crisis ended, a meeting was held in Montreal, Quebec to review the Oka Crisis, learn from it, and engage in conflict-prevention dialogue. The meeting organizers said that all stakeholders would be represented at this major gathering: all levels of government, representatives of the Aboriginal peoples, police and military personnel.

Among those invited to the meeting were Mohawk leaders from Akwesasne, who were asked to discuss their mediation centre and how they had resolved the conflict in their community. I was also invited to come and make a presentation on the general principles of ADR. As part of my presentation I talked about the importance of including everyone at the table. I added that although I did not doubt that the organizers of this Montreal meeting had in good faith sought to ensure all parties were present, I repeated: Is everyone at the table?

The next day, a call came in to the Akwesasne mediation centre asking if it was all right to quote what I'd said about including everyone at the table. The caller felt a particular group had been left out of the Montreal meeting and planned to write a letter of complaint to the federal government.

Sure enough, a letter to that effect found its way back to me through a senior official in the Department of Indian Affairs and Northern Development, who said that the letter had caused quite a fuss. However, the letter eventually led to a discussion about how problems in uniting the community could have been avoided if everyone had been invited to the table in Montreal.

Wherever there is disagreement, both sides want the opportunity to make their point of view known, and to do that they may resort to the courts, labour strikes, or wars. Gandhi, Martin Luther King, Jr. and Nelson Mandela are among those who have advocated non-violent civil disobedience, while others in the past have shut down

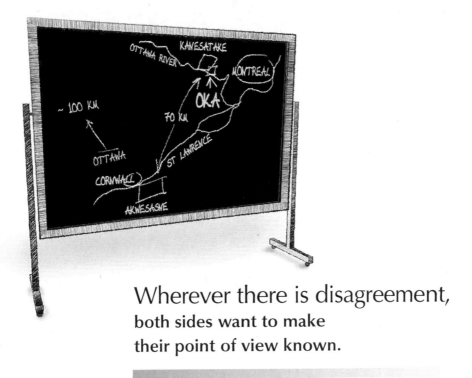

## Wherever there is disagreement,
**both sides want to make
their point of view known.**

highways, or taken their protests to the streets in marches, demonstrations or violence. Underlying all of these actions is the desire for negotiation.

The movie *The Negotiator* (1998, Warner Bros., dir. by F. Gary Gray) tells the story of a skilled police negotiator (Samuel L. Jackson) who is framed for murder and desperately tries to tell his side of the story. In one telling scene, the negotiator stands at an open window, fully armed, with a helicopter hovering above, and shouts: "I want to be heard!" At the heart of this story is a simple principle: Listen to all points of view.

## SOME LESSONS

● Always leave an empty chair at the table for those already involved who come and go, and for those who have not yet arrived, or for those who still influence us, such as those who have passed away. It's difficult to always ask, "Who else should be at the table?" but it's far more difficult to deal with the aftermath of exclusion.

● No one has the right or authority to impose a solution on others or even to enforce a process on others; historically, this is a deep-rooted conflict with Aboriginal peoples and other cultures around the world that saw colonists force them to adopt their Western form of democracy. In the Mohawk territory of Akwesasne the traditional people celebrate Jake Fire Day every May 1 in tribute to the Mohawk chief known as Jake Fire who died in 1899 resisting the imposition of the band system under the *Indian Advancement Act* of 1884. The police were later exonerated and other Mohawks arrested for interfering with the election. This perhaps helps explain why there is so much resistance to outsiders and the imposition of their views on the ancient cultures.

As I learned from Professor Ronald Fisher, "Before you talk about the issues, talk about how you will talk about the issues." Hence the need for everyone to be invited to the table and to be given the opportunity to find the common ground that will form the basis of their cooperation.

● When the war chief returned to Akwesasne, he told me many things that have remained with me all these years. One is that their Peace Maker had taught them to bury their guns under the Tree of Peace; another was a teaching from an elder that "each culture is like a flower and the world should be a beautiful bouquet in which all people and all things are interconnected." Finally, I was fascinated with his view of ADR: as a revelation from the Creator to the "white man," or Western society, to help bridge better communications with Aboriginal societies and their ancient process of decision by consensus. This insight helped guide the efforts in Akwesasne.

- The table has many cultural, historical and even biblical associations with acceptance and camaraderie, and it can be applied to many situations to give everyone an equal say. Promoting the idea of a table can often encourage the participation of others who may be feeling left out. This goes for any situation—work, family, community, local, international, and even in play! From history I have learned that our modern world requires more inclusive processes, like the table, to prevent, manage and solve conflict.

- Ultimately, no final solution can be sustainable unless everyone's point of view is considered.

# 2 IS YOUR HOUSE IN ORDER?

*Why make things difficult when,
with a little bit of effort,
we can make them impossible?*

BEFORE MAY 1990 I knew nothing about the Mohawk territory of Akwesasne except what I'd read in the papers. All I knew was that two people had been murdered when violence erupted in the territory in late April, and that the Canadian side of the territory had subsequently been evacuated to Cornwall, Ontario.

Just days after the evacuation, as the fighting continued at Akwesasne, I received a call from my friend and colleague, the legal counsel for the Mohawk Council of Akwesasne, asking if I would meet with Mohawk leaders in Cornwall to try to mediate a solution. At the time I was the executive director of the Canadian Institute of Conflict Resolution (CICR).

**I realized immediately that my attire would label me an outsider.**

I agreed to go to Cornwall, but told my friend I knew absolutely nothing about the issues or the source of the conflict. He then gave me some background into the complexities of this region: The Mohawk nation, part of the six-nation Iroquois

Confederacy, or the *Hotinonshonni,* had long ago been one large unified territory along the St. Lawrence River. With the arrival of the Europeans and the establishment of two separate countries, the territory had ended up split into two reserves: Akwesasne, located in both Ontario and Quebec, and St. Regis in the state of New York. Over time both the U.S. and Canadian governments had imposed Western-style elected governments on the Mohawks, so the territory was now governed by three

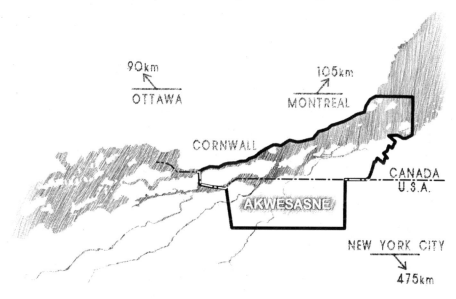

separate bodies: the elected Mohawk Council of Akwesasne (MCA) on the Canadian side; the elected St. Regis Mohawk Tribal Council on the U.S. side; and the self-governing traditional Longhouse chiefs, who refused to recognize the two elected councils because of their affiliation with Western democracies. Given their history, the Mohawk people were suspicious of any outsider, and for good reason.

My friend told me that the longstanding political turbulence over the governance of the territory had been magnified in recent years by continuing clashes between the territory's various factions. As the traditional way of life had diminished, income from gambling had increased, which had resulted in sometimes violent confrontations involving pro- and anti-gambling camps and law enforcement. One faction, known as the Warrior Society, or *Rotisken'rakéhte* in Mohawk, was particularly controversial because of its nationalistic tendencies and suspected paramilitary associations. Within the traditional *Hotinonshonni* culture the role of the *Rotisken'rakéhte* was to guard and protect the community. I remembered hearing about the Warrior Society's involvement at Oka, Quebec, where the Mohawks had erected a barricade to stop the expansion of a golf course onto land they considered sacred. At the time I did not understand all the links between these events but knew there were connections.

That brief overview of the background was all I took with me as I drove to Cornwall that day. I didn't have any idea what I was getting into or with whom I would be meeting. And neither did I know that I was about to begin an assignment as a conflict resolution consultant in Akwesasne that would eventually last two years.

When I arrived in Cornwall, my friend, the lawyer for MCA, introduced me to the grand chief and other leaders. Soon there was a call for assembly and we headed to a large auditorium. Hundreds of people had gathered and not a single chair was empty. The grand chief introduced me as someone he'd met through their lawyer, and told the crowd I had some things to say about conflict resolution. Without warning the grand chief and my lawyer friend left the hall, and there I was, all alone in front of a huge audience. I later learned that this kind of initiation by fire is part of the culture.

The silence was awkward as I stood before them. I noticed that every person in the audience wore casual or Native clothing, and I was suddenly self conscious about my business suit that seemed so formal and so Western.

I realized immediately that my attire would undoubtedly label me an outsider, so I introduced myself and told them of my Middle Eastern ancestry. Had I known I would be speaking with them, I said, I would have worn something more appropriate, maybe even an Arab outfit, and I would have driven a camel, not a car. There were some chuckles in the audience, and I felt some loosening of the tension and unease.

When I asked if anyone wanted to share anything about their situation, there was another long silence that seemed to stretch for several minutes. I decided I would wait for them and not try to fill the void with the sound of my own voice. If these people would so honour me, I wanted to hear their voices and feel their pain and their anger.

"Why do you care about us?" a voice demanded from the audience, shattering the silence.

That was a fascinating start that touched my heart. I told them how much I would appreciate knowing that others cared for my children and grandchildren, and how much I wished I could help the people in my father's homeland of Lebanon, where the recent civil war had killed so many and destroyed so much.

One of the key principles in any mediation is that the people involved in the dispute must find their own solution, and I sensed that for this group that principle would be particularly important. And so I sought to reassure them of what I was there to do. I told them how I was guided by a phrase I'd once heard, that a wise person realizes they have nothing new to offer the world. For me, I added, that meant that all we can do is share our experiences. I explained that when outsiders are asked to intervene in a dispute, the outsiders are not to take credit for any solution since that belongs to the people who are involved. But we first needed to find out what the situation was and determine if anything could be done to improve it.

I asked again if anyone wanted to share their experiences concerning the events in their community. This time the dialogue began—it was cordial and at times emotional, and throughout the morning more and more people participated. At the lunch break several people came over to thank me for coming, and expressed hope that a conflict resolution approach from the outside could help the community work out things. At the end the Mohawk leaders and the MCA lawyer came and spoke with me. The grand chief said that there seemed to be enough interest to take the next step. What would that be?

**"Why do you care about us?" a voice demanded from the audience.**

I told him that I and other representatives from the CICR would conduct a confidential active listening exercise with the community so that we could hear many different views of the situation. But as it turned out, the active listening exercise could not begin until a colleague and I were cleared by government, police and military officials, a process that involved many intense sessions with various agencies over many weeks.

From those sessions I vividly remember one particular exchange with a federal official. "The government has been trying for years to find a solution for that situation in Akwesasne," he said. "Nothing's going to change, although everyone would like to think it could."

"I was taught by very wise and experienced people in ADR that it's not up to outsiders to find a solution," I replied. "The people themselves must be given an opportunity and a process to find their common ground."

"Yeah, but what could that common ground possibly be?" the official asked.

"That's the point," I said. "None of us knows the answer to that question, and really it's none of our business. The purpose is to listen to what the people have to say and talk to the different groups. From that, the common ground will emerge. But nothing will work unless the community is given a chance to create a process for itself, based on its traditions. Only they can do it."

After several weeks of being thoroughly investigated, we finally received the green light to proceed with the active listening exercise, and we returned to Akwesasne to set up meetings with numerous individuals and groups from the community. At the end of the two-week exercise one common idea had indeed emerged: the traditional teaching of the seventh generation, which is based on the idea that the Mohawk people were to be mindful of the consequences of their actions down to the seventh generation beyond themselves.

## One common desire had emerged: the traditional teaching of the seventh generation.

I was absorbed by this teaching. Imagine being mindful that every action could affect a generation you will not live to see. What a responsibility and what better way to be conscious of your legacy. I was amazed that even amidst the deep-seated civil strife in this divided community all sides were unified around one idea: that they wanted the next generations to be better off. This ancient wisdom—spiritual, universal and practical all at the same time—was the common ground upon which they could build. Our report recommended that the Mohawk territory establish its own mediation centre, a process that would allow the community to help itself.

After this recommendation was approved, the next stage was to hold a second round of interviews and meetings in the territory. In this process I was guided by another important principle of mediation, which was to involve everyone in the process and allow everyone's voice to be heard.

This proved to be a major sticking point that nearly derailed the entire process. The Mohawk leaders that we were talking to at the time were determined to control whom we talked to, and they specifically wanted to exclude the Warrior Society. To preserve the integrity of the process, the conflict resolution team had determined that everyone had to be involved in the process, and we indicated that we would have to withdraw if that condition could not be met. (For more detailed information on this aspect, please see the opening chapter, "Is everyone at the table?")

My colleague and I finally received clearance to talk freely with everyone. We first spent months talking with groups and individuals supporting the Mohawk leadership, and then invested many more months meeting with supporters of the Warrior Society. When I returned to the community after these Warrior Society meetings the MCA chiefs summoned me to explain where I had been. It

**I had to find a way to communicate the importance of honouring the process.**

was clear that I had to find a way to communicate the importance of honouring the process we had agreed on.

I had seen the significance of images in the culture, so when it came time for our meeting I decided to illustrate my point visually. I went to the flip chart and drew a picture of a house with many rooms, and then told the chiefs a story that I had come up with about a family that lived in a house...

The family was so bitterly divided that members were living in separate rooms on three different floors: the basement, the ground floor and the upper floor. One family member finally asked for help in mediating a solution, and when the mediator arrived he went through the house, room by room, to meet all the family members. Many of them were suspicious of the stranger at first, but eventually, after many meetings the mediator was able to get past the mistrust. With the

assistance of the mediator, the family members living on the ground floor slowly reconciled with those living upstairs, and they decided to hold a great feast to celebrate the end of their fighting. However, they did not invite any family members from the basement.

When the mediator asked why those in the basement had not been included in the celebration, he was told that those in the basement were troublemakers and were not welcome in the family. The mediator insisted that everyone had to be at the table to celebrate, and went into the basement to meet these other family members and hear their story.

When the mediator returned upstairs and saw that the festivities were about to begin, he reminded those at the dinner table that the family gathering was missing several members, but the leaders were adamant that those in the basement were not welcome.

The mediator pleaded with everyone to rethink, and said that if the excluded members in the basement were excluded from the dinner, they would blow up the house during the celebration.

I used this visual image and this imaginary story to make an important point: a process had been established to help the community find its own solution and put its own house in order, and the process required the participation of everyone. If the process were not followed, or if any part of the community were barred from participating, those who were excluded would find another way to make their voices heard. The visual image seemed to resonate with the chiefs, and it seemed they realized the potential consequences if others tried to hijack the process.

There were still many challenges ahead, but the community moved forward with the establishment of the mediation centre, called *Sken Nen Kowa*—an organization for peace in Akwesasne. The traditional teachings, combined with the principles of ADR and conflict resolution, seemed to strengthen the Mohawk leadership and give them the endurance they needed to survive the destabilizing forces.

After months of negotiations the various factions finally gathered at a Cornwall hotel for their first meeting, which had one purpose: to discuss implementing a rumour control system to reduce the violence within the community. This was an idea from my colleague Tom Colosi to prevent the process from being disrupted by destabilizing forces, troublemakers, misunderstandings, or inadvertent information. The idea was that each faction, and each police force, would designate a representative. Before anyone acted on information circulating in the community they would check it out with the other representatives and the police to be sure the situation was not worsened by incorrect information, gossip or false rumours planted to stir up trouble.

The idea resonated with the Mohawk people, one of whom called this a modern application of a traditional method their ancestors had used to verify information. The police were intrigued and supportive of the concept too, as was the ambassador from South Africa whom I later met through a colleague. The ambassador told me about a gunfight in South Africa in which dozens of people were killed. The battle had started when someone reacted to a sound that was assumed to be a gunshot, and the violence escalated from there. He told me that the "gunshot" was probably a tire blowout, and the carnage could have been prevented with a rumour control system.

## The rumour control system was one step toward putting the house in order.

This system did help with conflict prevention and maintenance, and allowed the community to take a step toward putting its house in order. It was also a unique way to build on the common ground that we had identified at the beginning of the process: ensuring a better future for the next seven generations.

After the mediation centre was successfully established, a leader of the Warrior Society told me that he believed success had been possible because, for the first time in 100 years, the Mohawks in Akwesasne had been given the opportunity to do something by and for themselves.

### SOME LESSONS

● I was told that every police force and intelligence agency studied me every which way from Sunday; in fact, I interacted with all the police forces on the territory in one way or another. I learned much later that these agencies were looking for my personal agenda, but could not find anything other than my desire to help. Because of my Lebanese background some thought I had ties to a casino owner of Middle Eastern ancestry. Others accused me of being manipulated by both sides of the dispute, speculated that I was a government spy, or said that I was simply naïve. No matter what issue you get involved in, there are always two factors at work: what you get from the outside, and what you give from inside yourself.

● Being neutral is not easy; some say it's impossible. By the time I arrived in Akwesasne another well-known peace group from outside the territory had already been there but the key mediator eventually took a side and it hurt the process integrity. That person said it was not possible to stay neutral. This was a lesson for me. As we began the process of establishing the mediation centre a Mohawk elder asked me how it would be possible for me to *not* form an opinion about who was right or wrong. "I'm on the side of the community, not on the side of any one faction," I told her. "My fight is for the mediation process, not on how the issues are settled. I will make no decisions; your community will decide by consensus how it will proceed." I found a lesson in becoming aware of the role I was playing.

● The first step in mediation is to include everyone at the negotiating table; the second step is to pay attention to what everyone has to say. Not paying attention to everyone's interest can eventually be more damaging than the challenge of including everyone in the decision making.

● During the listening exercise, everyone we talked to—regardless of politics or other beliefs—agreed that there was one person in particular that they could work with. That person eventually became the executive director of the mediation centre. After the centre was successfully established—against all odds and despite many dire predictions—the board of directors and executive director were invited to present at a workshop being held concurrently with an international conference on conflict resolution and peacemaking in the U.S. I had been asked to attend their session, which was so popular that there was an overflow crowd.

To my surprise, the executive director called my name and asked me to stand up. She said, "When

Ernie came to Akwesasne he did not pretend to bring in any solutions or answers to our problems. He brought himself and some ideas for how we could design our own process to heal our community. What essentially happened is that we were reminded to go back to the basics, to go back and relearn what our Peace Maker and elders had taught us long ago, which we had forgotten or were not applying. That is what made the difference in Akwesasne."

This was a stunning insight that visibly affected the audience, and there were front-page headlines about the Akwesasne presentation. It was a powerful reminder of a universal truth: to go from disorder to order, start by going back to the basics.

I have applied that teaching often, and it's amazing what people discover when they go back to the basics in their own lives, whatever the setting, culture or religion. It reminds me of Robert Fulghum's 1988 book, *All I Really Need to Know I Learned in Kindergarten* (which has been called "a guide for global leadership"). In life so often we make things more complicated than they need to be, and as a result the conflicts become harder to resolve. Maybe we can help end the disputes, and put our house in order, by focusing on the basic principles that sustain us.

# 3 HOW DO YOU BRING RELIEF TO THE SITUATION?

*Whether you are working or playing,*
*during the day or at night, if you're not having*
*fun, you're not doing it right.*

AFTER SPENDING MUCH TIME in Akwesasne after 1990, I befriended the executive director of the mediation centre and her family.

During a weekend visit to Akwesasne, her two grandsons, then aged about 8 and 10 years old, asked me to take them to the new community bakery near the St. Lawrence River. It was a bright Sunday morning, and when we arrived at the bakery about a dozen people were sitting at the small tables. Displayed near the cash register were packages of cookies, $1 per dozen, and the children immediately asked if they could have some cookies. Each boy wanted a different type of cookie; one wanted chocolate chip while the other said he preferred oatmeal raisin. Each package had only one type of cookie, however, and I felt neither boy really needed a dozen cookies. Thus, I saw this as a challenge to give each boy what he wanted.

**It occurred to me that this was an ideal teachable moment in conflict resolution.**

It occurred to me that this was an ideal teachable moment in conflict resolution, and a simple situation to show the boys how to resolve a matter in a fair way.

I turned to the bakery manager who was waiting patiently for our order. "Could you please give me two packages of cookies, with six chocolate chip cookies in one package and six oatmeal raisin cookies in the other?"

He smiled and nodded.

For the benefit of the boys, who were intently watching this exchange, I added, "That way both boys will get the type of cookie they want, and it will only cost one dollar."

While the bakery assistant was repackaging the cookies I looked around and saw that everyone in the bakery was now watching this episode unfold. My ego was in high gear, and I felt that now everyone could learn the lesson that I was about to teach. I was priding myself for coming up with this idea of taking an everyday situation and turning it into an opportunity to provide a profound lesson.

I paid the dollar and took the two newly wrapped packages of cookies, six chocolate chip in one hand and six oatmeal raisin in the other. With the deal done, the contract completed, and all the arrangements finalized in view of everyone in the shop, I was beaming as I prepared to utter profound words that were sure to inspire much praise and nodding of heads.

Glancing around at the attentive audience, I held out the cookies to the boys and said loudly, so that no one would miss the message I was about to share: "Now children, what have you learned from this?"

I could feel the sense of expectation in the room as we waited for the boys to provide some great insight into this amazing life lesson.

"Well, Ernie," the younger boy said, taking the package of cookies from me, "we learned that you are cheap!"

## Everyone in the bakery was now watching this episode unfold.

The assembled group of people roared with laughter, and I couldn't help but laugh along with them all.

Of all of the stories that I have shared, this one seems to generate the greatest response, and it never loses its freshness. This story brought much amusement to the family and others in Akwesasne, and made my relationship with them even closer.

Two years before this episode, when I first came to Akwesasne, the Mohawk Council of Akwesasne (MCA) agreed to bring me, as part of the Canadian Institute for Conflict Resolution, into their community to help settle their civil strife. After several months of conducting initial sessions in the community I was about to begin the conflict resolution consulting, and I was brought into a room where the MCA lawyer and several other community leaders all sat around the perimeter. The grand chief and I sat together at a table in the middle.

The grand chief told me that the MCA leaders felt I had the spirit and the strength to perform this task, but I needed to learn one very important point before I began. He said he would pass down this information the way it had been passed down to others before me, through the wisdom and traditions of the ancestors. He asked me to listen carefully so I could learn this lesson of their people. I sat respectfully, noting that all in the room were solemn, and I sensed that I was about to hear something of tremendous importance. He began the lesson:

*A mother and daughter rose early every Saturday morning to fish at a nearby lake. Almost every week they saw another mother and daughter also fishing. Sometimes the other women were on the far side of the lake, and other times they fished on the near side, close to the mother and daughter. But no matter which side the other women were on they always caught fish, but the mother and daughter never caught anything. After several weeks of this, the mother and daughter decided to visit the home of the other women to find out their secret.*

*When they knocked the other mother answered the door. "My mother and I are curious," said the daughter."How do you and your daughter know every week which side of the lake to fish on?"*

At this point I perked up with interest, as I sensed the answer to that question must be the lesson. I straightened up in my chair, anticipating that I was about to learn one of the ancient Aboriginal teachings that I'd heard so much about.

*The second mother invited them in, saying, "The answer to your question rests with my daughter," and led them to a room at the back of the house. When she opened the door, the mother and daughter were quite taken aback to see the other daughter lying under a blanket with her husband, both obviously in their natural state. The guests overcame their embarrassment and the daughter said: "My mother and I wish to know how you and your mother know which side of the lake to fish on."*

Once again I sat in suspense, waiting for the teaching to

be revealed through the answer to this fascinating question. The room was very quiet, everyone intensely listening to the grand chief tell this story.

*The other daughter lifted the blanket slightly and peered underneath. "Early each Saturday morning I look under this sheet. If it is lying to the left, we fish on the left side of the lake, but if it is lying to the right, we fish on the right side of the lake."*

**I straightened up, anticipating I was about to learn an ancient Aboriginal teaching.**

I was a little bewildered at that moment, and wondered if this was really a joke, but the grand chief was very serious, as was everyone in the room, so I figured that these deep teachings were passed down in ways that I was not accustomed to. So I banished that thought and waited for the rest of the story so I could learn the lesson of the people that the grand chief wanted me to understand.

*So the mother and daughter thanked the young woman for sharing her secret and left the house. They quickly realized they had forgotten to ask perhaps the most important question of all, so they returned to the house, knocked on the door and explained why they were back. Once again the mother led them to her daughter's room.*

The grand chief stopped at this point. "Ernie, do you know the important question they forgot to ask?"

I was stumped, wondering if I was missing something and worried that I was about to fail the final test. I struggled to think of what that question could be.

"Honestly, I don't know," I said sheepishly, feeling that perhaps I would not be asked to continue in my role since I could not figure out the answer to this very important question.

"All right," the grand chief continued, "let me complete the story so you can learn the lesson."

I decided that even if they told me I could not stay,

at least I would be honoured to learn this lesson from the grand chief, so I sat up straight and listened closely.

*The mother and daughter stood at the bedroom door and asked the other daughter if they could ask one more question, the most important question of all. The daughter agreed. "So our question is, which side of the lake do you fish on if it's lying neither to the right or the left?"*

I was now fully alert as I waited for the words of wisdom to finally be revealed...

## I sat in suspense, waiting for the teaching to be revealed.

*The daughter on the bed lifted the sheet again, and answered, "If it is lying neither to the left nor to the right, we do not go fishing that day!"*

Well, every single person in the room laughed, including the grand chief, and I realized that I had been had, but the story was so well delivered that I could not help but truly enjoy the experience.

The grand chief said that he wanted me to understand that no matter how dangerous or violent their community was at that moment, with two unsolved murders and guns everywhere, the people in the community would always keep their sense of humour. He wanted me to fully appreciate the importance of that quality as I went into the community to hear what the people from all sides had to say.

This turned out to be another fine part of the preparation for this intervention. It was important to keep a sense of humour as the conflict resolution efforts were being pursued in Akwesasne.

### SOME LESSONS

- Humility is so important in any communication; otherwise ego, arrogance or indifference can creep in. Being humble and being humbled are enlightening events.

- Be prepared for anything; expect the unexpected. Be mindful that "to everything there is a season" (Ecclesiastes 3:1). That passage from Ecclesiastes 3 is one of the finest pieces of literature, in my view. It also says there is "a time to weep, and a time to laugh, a time to mourn, and a time to dance." In life, we need to learn many dance steps.

- Sometimes we take life too seriously, and unless we "lighten up," our load becomes too heavy to carry. And just like when you have too much baggage for the plane, you end up paying for that extra weight! A sense of humour can help lighten your load and bring a good balance to life's challenges. Often  humour can bring relief or even joy to a situation and help prevent the situation from getting worse.

- Sometimes the humour we use can offend others, and we must be careful what we say, how we say it, and to whom we say it. For example, long ago I was an instructor in the bar admission course on negotiations with a class of about 20 students. One morning I told a joke that seemed to fit, but aware that some in the room could take offence, I first carefully prefaced it to put it in context. At the break one of the female students told me she was not coming back to the class because she was insulted and offended at my joke. I tried to explain that I was sensitive to that, which is why I had prefaced it as I had. She said that had not made any difference, and she was leaving class to complain to the director of the program and to ask to be placed in a different class. I said that I understood but asked if she wouldn't mind sharing her complaints with the class after the break since I felt it would not be appropriate for me to speak for her. She kindly agreed, and when she was finished speaking to the class I explained to everyone that it had not been my intention to offend, and I apologized and said I had learned yet another lesson. That dialogue with her became a basis for explaining the negotiation principles we were covering that morning, and she remained in the class.

# 4 WHO BENEFITS FROM CONFLICT?

*War is good business for the few; peace is better business for the many.*

ONE DAY I was asked to speak to a group of 125 correctional officers at a prison as part of a professional development day.

Just minutes before I was scheduled to address the group, the organizer told me that correctional officers were concerned that if alternative dispute resolution (ADR) and restorative justice actually worked, fewer people would go to prison, and their careers as correctional officers would be jeopardized.

**The prospect of fewer inmates could be a threat to the entire bureaucracy.**

It's not hard to imagine how the prospect of fewer inmates could be quite a threat to the entire bureaucracy. Since Canada's overall recidivism rate of between 45 and 75 percent[1] is providing a steady clientele for the correctional service, if fewer people are in prison, fewer people will also return to prison. Critics

---

1 These statistics are drawn from recent research conducted by Vern White, Chief of Police in Ottawa, Ontario, Canada. His research shows that although recidivism rates in Canada are subject to various factors, including jurisdiction and cultural group, they generally range between 45 percent and 75 percent in the five years following release from incarceration.

say that with a law-and-order agenda being pursued the way it is, the prison system is one business that is set to thrive well into the future—so why fix it?

The warning from the organizer was not surprising, but he delivered it just a few minutes before I was to take the podium. All of a sudden the conditions had changed, and now I was about to speak to an audience that probably didn't even want to hear what I had to say. I was not entirely surprised to hear their concern, as I had already seen time and again how the philosophy and pragmatism of ADR challenges the underlying assumptions of many institutions and affects individuals—but the immediate problem was this: how could I address the fear in the audience?

I stepped to the podium and looked out at the sea of faces. I admired the courage of the organizer in putting this subject at the top of agenda. But what could I say to these correctional officers? How could I draw their attention to this important subject yet also speak to their concerns?

> How could I draw attention to this subject yet speak to their concerns?

I did the only thing that I could. I decided at that moment to deviate from my text and go back to basics by talking about a universal truth.

"Good morning," I said. "I want to begin by complimenting you for including this topic as a theme. I understand there is some fear in this room around what ADR will mean to your jobs."

I noticed a shuffling of papers and people shifting in their seats. *Good,* I thought. *At least I've got their attention.*

"But I'm here to tell you the other side of this issue," I continued. "I want to tell you that it's incumbent on you to learn all you can about ADR, and particularly about restorative justice. Because if you don't learn about these important topics, that's when your jobs will be in jeopardy and your careers adversely affected."

The audience was silent, and every eye was fixed on me. This unexpected beginning had clearly intrigued the audience.

That morning I never got to my carefully prepared notes. Instead I talked to the group about the human and economic costs of conflict, and how institutions of all types seem to have lost sight of their mandate, which is to serve their constituents and not themselves. This theme is the same in all disciplines—the issue is universal and the list of examples endless.

Early in my ADR journey, I learned the expression *cui bono*, which is Latin for "who benefits." My comments that morning were not meant to condemn anyone but rather to raise awareness that institutions are not intrinsically benevolent, and they do not always benefit those they are supposed to serve. We must be aware that by protecting their own self-serving interests, institutions may actually be harming the best interests of those they are supposed to serve, including families, the wider community, and indeed society in general.

After my address, the organizer was enthusiastic in his praise. "You said exactly the right thing," he said as he pumped my hand.

The representatives in the audience from the John Howard and Elizabeth Fry societies also offered positive feedback. More significant, though, was that a few correctional officers approached me and commented that they had never thought about the issue in those terms and understood why it would be important.

Vern White, the current chief of police here in Ottawa (and whose M.A. thesis was on the topic of restorative justice), is on the record as saying that increasing and repeating prison populations are a sign that the system of corrections, policing and courts are failing, not succeeding. Chief White has said that we need to deal with the deep-rooted social problems that give rise to these problems. Ordinary citizens already know this, and grassroots efforts are needed to address them for long-term gain. We need to begin by educating ourselves about ADR, or at least unlearning some of the habits taught to us from childhood through adulthood. We need to point the way, not a finger.

## Institutions of all types seem to have lost sight of their mandate.

One of the 260 shows I did for the weekly ADR radio program on CHIN radio was titled "Cancer: It's about a cure, it's about time." The program addressed alternative cancer treatments that reduce the need for pharmaceutical drugs and radical surgeries. These new approaches do not eliminate drugs and surgeries but are aimed at finding a balance. Both the literature and empirical evidence show that when appropriate, many cancers can be treated or managed without intrusive interventions that often do not benefit the patient.

The less intrusive approach holds true for litigation, war, and many other areas of human activity. There is widespread suspicion that the economics of conflict serve the needs of many other agendas. But most of the population has a common sense appreciation of other ways that will better serve the greater good. We already embrace the logic of practising fire prevention and dental and medical prevention, so why not conflict prevention?

Brian Lennox, a former judge who is now the executive director of the Canadian Judicial Institute, once said that we must change our attitude so that we are not obstructed by the fear of change. I believe we would do well by following this advice.

## SOME LESSONS

- Be open to alternative thinking in every discipline; encourage new ideas and new ways of doing things, and don't be afraid to challenge assumptions. As noted educator Edward de Bono has said, don't just bring in an untried approach and throw out the old; have the courage to try some new approaches but keep existing methods in place and improve upon them.[2] Don't be like the stones on Easter Island, frozen in time and looking in only one direction. Racehorses wear blinders to keep them looking straight ahead, but unless you are a racehorse you should take off your blinders! As I always told my children, look around you, even behind you when you go through a door to make sure you are not slamming it on someone coming behind you. That kind of ordinary approach that can lead to extraordinary changes in the way we think.

- Major changes are often accompanied by fear. One well-known example from history concerns the Luddites, the British textile workers who in the early 19th century destroyed the mechanical textile looms they feared

---

2 Dr. de Bono made this comment at the American Bar Association Mediation and Education Conference, April 8–10, 1988.

were replacing their jobs. But it might help to keep in mind that the change you are resisting may ultimately be in your best interests.

● When you feel uncomfortable about what is happening around you, try asking "Who is benefiting?" and see where that leads you. Perhaps it will shed light on self-serving agendas of individuals or institutions. I have found that asking "Who benefits from the conflict?" leads to an entirely different conversation and perspective on the circumstances.

● Always be vigilant (without being a vigilante) about ensuring that people and organizations are truly serving those they have been entrusted to care for, and are not just looking out for themselves.

# 5 IS BITING BACK THE BEST RESPONSE?

*World peace through inner peace.*

ONE DAY I ARRIVED in Akwesasne to meet the Chair of the Akwesasne Chamber of Commerce. As I pulled into the empty lot outside his building I noticed no one else was around—not a person, not a car. A gas station was in front of his building, but no one was outside.

As I walked towards the door I heard a fierce sound. I turned to see an enormous dog racing towards me, barking ferociously. He was at the far end of the empty

**The solution, I decided, was to stop worrying about external events.**

lot, and at first he seemed quite far away, but he was snarling and highly agitated as he charged towards me. Many years before I'd had a frightening experience with a dog that had come at me out of nowhere, and I'd tried to outrun him. Thankfully, the dog's lead had been just short enough to prevent him from attacking me. The experience had remained with me all these years.

Fear immediately gripped me as I sensed that this time I was not going to be so lucky; I was about to be attacked. Knowing I had only seconds to figure out what to do, I quickly decided that this time I wouldn't try to outrun the dog. My instinct was to defend myself and fight back, but I knew that would probably antagonize the dog and make him attack me more viciously.

The solution, I decided, was to stop worrying about the external events happening around me. Instead, I centred myself and focused on what was happening inside myself. I turned toward the dog, arms outstretched to welcome and embrace him as a friend.

As the dog came closer, and I could see his vicious teeth and burning eyes, I began speaking to the dog in my thoughts. I realize this sounds rather odd, but I did not utter any words out loud. I can only describe it as a dialogue inside my head with the dog.

*I have come to this territory for peace for the community,* I said to him through my thoughts. *I am not an enemy and I do not intend to fight with you or challenge you.*

The dog was still coming straight for me, growling and barking aggressively, but I remained calm and continued my inner dialogue.

*I understand your natural instinct to attack and protect your community from strangers, but I am not a stranger. I was invited here by the People. I respect the environment and all of the animals in Akwesasne.*

I did all I could to project these thoughts, hoping and praying that the dog would somehow sense my peace.

I consciously kept repeating these tranquil thoughts, all

the while breathing in and out deeply and slowly, consciously willing myself into a quiet inner peace.

I was aware that the dog was very close. Suddenly he leaped at me, and right before my face I saw his bared teeth coming at me. By now, however, my fear was gone, and I reminded myself that I had no conflict with this animal.

This was both a strange and satisfying feeling, since I truly had to let go and trust the teachings of this Aboriginal land, where I had learned about their belief that all peoples and all things in creation are interconnected.

Then the dog and I looked at each other eye to eye, but at that moment the only thing I felt was serenity. The next instant, the dog sank his teeth into my jacket, ripping the leather. I didn't move. The dog then clamped his teeth around my right ankle bone, chomping relentlessly into my skin.

I wanted to scream but I decided to stay quiet, stand perfectly still and not try to shake him off. At that point I began to feel I was going to be OK. If the dog had wanted to seriously injure me, he would have already done so. I sensed his aggression had subsided, and that he would not continue to attack me.

**I realized the choice I made would affect both myself and the dog.**

Three Mohawk men began running towards me from different directions, shouting words of encouragement.

"Stay still!" yelled one.

"We're coming!" shouted the second.

"Don't worry!" said the third.

A sense of relief flooded me as I saw my rescuers. They rebuked the dog in English and Mohawk, and immediately the dog obeyed. The men led him away without a fuss, nodding wordlessly to me as they left. I nodded back my thanks and headed inside to see Paul, the man I was scheduled to meet.

"Ernie, what happened?" Paul said, rising from his desk, concern on his face. "I heard the commotion and looked out the window but all I saw was the dog being led away."

I told him the story. "You know, at first I was quite frightened, but I realized immediately the choice I made would affect both myself and the dog."

> I consciously kept willing myself into a quiet inner peace.

"I'm so sorry you were attacked, Ernie," Paul said. "Let me pay for your ruined leather jacket."

"Thank you, but that's not necessary," I said. "In fact, I should be paying you! I've just learned a priceless and valuable lesson that will stay with me for the rest of my life."

As Paul and I were talking, a middle-aged man walked in using crutches and wearing a cast that extended from his foot to above his knee.

"What happened to you?" Paul said.

"Stupid stray dogs!" the man said. "One of 'em attacked me, and when I tried to fight him off he came at me even harder."

Paul pointed to me. "Ernie here was also just attacked by one of those strays. His jacket is destroyed but he has no other injuries. You should have done what he did and not fight back."

## SOME LESSONS

- When someone attacks you, at whatever level, be mindful that your reaction could either worsen or improve the situation. Choose wisely.

- Before you react to aggression, hold back, even for a brief moment. You may find that other options come to mind for dealing with the aggression.

- Try stepping back from the situation to see the larger context; that is, try to see the whole forest and not just the tree that's staring you in the face. Often seeing the larger context will help you realize what effect your reaction will have on other people.

- Observe how others react to situations and use those experiences as a mirror to better see your own reactions. Use those experiences to learn to be calm. Remember that there are many non-violent options, such as civil disobedience, that can be used to defend yourself against aggression. Those who practice the martial art Akido learn to use the other person's energy to avoid causing harm while protecting themselves.

- Even when it looks like the situation will result in damage, be grateful in finding the humility in what happened, and see what resources come to assist you.

- Be mindful not only of the outside challenges staring you in the face but also of internal challenges that continue to snarl and growl at you.

- Dogs are usually seen as loyal, domesticated pets that form lifelong bonds with their owners. But just as dogs may occasionally bite their owners or attack someone they know, sometimes a person you know and trust will suddenly turn on you, double-cross you or stab you in the back.

- Facing a snarling dog is like facing fear. Is it better to face our fears, or to try and avoid them to the point of changing our life's path? One of my favourite movie scenes is from *The Silence of the Lambs* (1991, Orion

Pictures, dir. by Jonathan Demme) when the FBI agent, Clarice Starling (Jodie Foster) is forced to face her fears as she tracks down a serial killer. In a gripping scene, the killer stalking her in the dark cocks his gun, giving away his location, and she whirls around and kills him. It makes me think that once we identify our fear, it's better to turn around and face it.

● Could we deal more effectively with life's obstacles, stresses, suffering, and hardships if we could learn to be *less self-centred* and *more centred in ourselves?*

# 6 HOW DO YOU ACHIEVE HARMONY?

*Let your attitude determine how
you deal with your circumstances; don't let
your circumstances dictate your attitude.*

A COLLEAGUE WHO is a family mediator approached me about a well-known local women's chorus affiliated with an international association. For various reasons the chorus was fractured, with some issues between individual chorus members and others between the chorus members and the director. They had tried to sort out these issues themselves but the problems seemed to worsen with every weekly rehearsal. Adding to the urgency was the chorus' upcoming, sold-out Christmas concert with a celebrity guest singer.

**They clearly wanted to preserve what they had built and were willing to work hard.**

The much-anticipated annual concert seemed in jeopardy, as did the very existence of the chorus.

I offered to conduct an initial inquiry into the matter and determine whether I could conduct an appropriate intervention or suggest someone else better equipped to do so. A meeting with the chairperson of their executive committee was first, followed by a meeting with the entire committee. After a review of their bylaws and the international constitution of this chorus consortium, an intervention team was assembled to assist them in solving their disputes.

I attended their weekly rehearsals, sometimes with other mediators, and sometimes with a chorus member from a nearby U.S. chapter affiliated with the same international group. This chorus member not only had facilitation skills but also understood the dynamics of the chorus.

Whenever I am invited to contribute to a problem-solving exercise, I always seek to find a metaphor relevant to the group's purpose. The metaphor can be enlightening, and it often helps the group think about the problem-solving exercise in terms they can relate to.

Accordingly, the metaphor for this musical group was much clearer than for most. Each week after their rehearsal, I came into the room, thanked them for welcoming me into their world and, with an imaginary wave of my magical wand, announced that with their consent the rehearsal room was now transformed into the conflict resolution room. The purpose of the room had changed, but the objective was the same—to achieve harmony, not just in musical terms, but also with each other.

After attending so many of their rehearsals I could see the chorus members loved singing and were committed to the group. It occurred to me that their dedication to achieving harmony as singers could be a unifying principle in this mediation exercise. It was significant that they were all volunteers and sang with the group because they chose to, not because they had to. After so many years of singing together and establishing goodwill, they clearly wanted to preserve what they had built and, as with their music, they were willing to work hard to achieve their goal.

The first step in the problem-solving exercise was to conduct a confidential, written exercise in active listening, which allowed the group members to identify issues. They were given a choice whether to identify themselves or to give anonymous feedback, and about three-quarters of them chose to remain anonymous. From this exercise the mediation team produced a feedback report outlining the various issues and confirming that everyone wanted to work it out, save the chorus, and continue with the Christmas concert.

There were many different aspects to this mediation exercise, which had been designed by the committee and the group to suit their needs and their deadlines. In between our weekly sessions I met separately with some chorus members on particular interpersonal challenges that they were facing, and often during the group sessions separate sessions were held concurrently with different components of the chorus. At the same time a group dialogue was sometimes held that was facilitated by the member from the sister chorus.

As with any organization, some of the problems were systemic, and we were able to help identify the elements that needed fixing. Changes were made to the bylaws

that would help with conflict prevention in the future, and it was determined that these changes would also be of use to the international association as a whole. Sometimes it happens that a solution at one level benefits the entire system.

One night while waiting to go into the room with my magic make-believe conflict resolution wand, I noticed a gentleman sitting at a desk selling raffle tickets for a beautiful hand-knit afghan throw. To support the chorus I bought a number of tickets, but never told anyone that I had done so.

## The mediation saved not only the Christmas concert but also the chorus itself.

Later that evening, when the room had been transformed from a rehearsal space into a conflict resolution class, I summarized the mediation team's observations and analysis, suggesting a series of steps that would help them achieve harmony as a group so they could continue to share their music with each other and with their audiences. As a result, some changes were made to the concert line-up, and the Christmas concert went ahead as planned.

With much joy I attended the concert with my daughter, knowing the incredible efforts that the members had made to keep the chorus together and perform as a unified group. At the end they received a well-deserved standing ovation.

A week later a chorus member phoned to tell me that at the group's Christmas party my ticket had been drawn and that I had won the hand-knit throw. "We can't think of anyone more deserving than you, Ernie," she said. "We're all happy that you'll have this to remember what we accomplished together." To this day, that afghan throw reminds me what can be accomplished by a group when everyone has the right attitude and is determined to work through their issues.

Some time after this mediation, my colleague who had first contacted me about the chorus told me that the chorus members were convinced that the mediation had saved not only the Christmas concert but also the chorus itself. Since then, the chorus has reconciled fully and over the years has won awards at regional and international competitions.

This story about the chorus achieving harmony led me to think about how ADR metaphors are all around us, which further demonstrates that ADR is a universal truth. I have selected four examples of other metaphors:

### Trim Tab—Staying on course

Scientists from a prestigious national organization were required to attend a training session on a new harassment policy. Another presenter and I had were conducting these sessions, and it was clear to us that the scientists had little interest in this subject and felt it wasn't relevant to their high level of expertise. I decided to try using a metaphor to engage their interest, and recalled learning about a small component called a trim tab, a tiny piece attached to a rudder that stabilizes an airplane or ship and keeps it on course. Imagine the umpteen thousands of high-tech parts that must go into airplanes and ships, yet this tiny component keeps them on course. The trim tab is a fantastic part of these massive vessels and a phenomenal metaphor.

I asked if any scientists in the room were familiar with trim tabs, and one promptly said that was his area of specialization. I had only a superficial layperson's understanding, so I asked him to explain what trim tabs are and how they work. He was very knowledgeable and enthusiastic about his subject of expertise, and ended up giving the group a mini-lecture. When he was finished I explained that ADR is like a trim tab, and no matter how much knowledge individuals in an organization have or how sophisticated its members are, without a trim tab process for human interactions the organization would lose its way and go off course. This metaphor worked like a charm.

## The Trip—Locating the problem

In another case I was called into a huge hydroelectric company in a complex conflict resolution intervention involving a manager and an outside security guard. In preparing for the intervention, I asked people in the industry to explain how they dealt with breakdowns in the electrical distribution system. They showed me an enormous computer screen of the entire electrical grid and explained that if there was a problem and electricity was not being delivered to a particular place, the source of the problem, called the trip, could be identified on the screen. Once the trip was located, crews would be sent to work on the problem and get the electricity flowing again. So we used that metaphor of the trip to guide the intervention. Everyone knew what to do to find the trip, and what tools to use to improve interpersonal communication.

## Hypothalamus—The body's mediator

I was involved in a healthcare dispute resolution involving many types of medical personnel: doctors, nurses, health administrators, social workers, physiotherapists, and occupational therapists. I told the group they were like the human body, with every member playing an important role in keeping our systems functioning. I explained how I liked to use metaphors in dispute resolutions and asked them about the hypothalamus gland, which I'd read was like the mediator in our bodies. The group became very animated and excitedly launched into a fascinating discussion of how this tiny gland in the brain plays such a critical role in the functioning of our bodies. The hypothalamus is often called the master gland since it regulates many functions that are essential to our survival, including body temperature, appetite, digestion, blood pressure, sleep, and metabolic activity. After this discussion I reminded the healthcare team that the hypothalamus gland acts as a mediator to keep our bodies functioning properly, and suggested they use that metaphor to help define each person's place in the medical system. This helped the group reshape their dialogue.

## The ADR Editor—Staying in sync

Finally, my favourite metaphor relates to a trip to Los Angeles with a theatre director from Ottawa. We had been invited to meet with some people to discuss how mediation and conflict resolution could be portrayed in the entertainment industry. At one gathering I was introduced to a woman who said that she worked in movies as an ADR editor. I could hardly contain myself. "That's terrific!" I said. "I had no idea that Hollywood was already applying alternative dispute resolution!"

She looked bewildered. "I don't know what you mean," she replied. "What's alternative dispute resolution?"

After hearing my explanation she said that didn't describe her job at all, and explained that in movie production ADR stands for automated (or additional) dialogue replacement. In this process the actors are called back during post-production to rerecord dialogue that wasn't recorded properly during the shoot, or that has too much interference from background noise. The ADR editor supervises this rerecording process and precisely syncs the newly recorded lines to the actors' mouth movements on film. This is a very important sound technique in movie production.

I was elated. "Thank you for that!" I told her. "You have just given me the best metaphor for what ADR really means!"

As I see it, ADR in the movies is a process that fixes the dialogue and syncs the words with the actors' movements so that the movie makes sense. Alternative dispute resolution has the same purpose: to fix communication processes and to help people stay in sync and make sense of the movie of life. This ADR metaphor fits so perfectly

## ADR metaphors are all around us.

that whenever I go to a movie with someone I insist we stay and read the credits. I do this for two reasons; first, so that we can appreciate that making movies takes a team effort and that many people besides the actors are needed; and second, to take note of the ADR editor and remind ourselves of the universal importance of staying in sync and in harmony with each other.

## SOME LESSONS:

- Imagine listening to a band, orchestra or chorus and hearing that one musician is out of tune. Or maybe you can recall watching a sport or activity, such as synchronized swimming, cheerleading, acrobatics, or a marching band, when one member of the group is out of sync. Have you ever noticed it takes only one performer to throw the entire performance off track? The same is true in interpersonal communication. As long as people are in step with others, life continues harmoniously, but when something goes off track there needs to be a process to remedy the situation. This simple, universal truth has anchored my ADR journey.

- Consider the dysfunction or danger that can result if people are not in sync. The Snowbirds, officially known as Canadian Forces 431 Air Demonstration Squadron, fly in perfect formation while performing incredible aerobatic feats. Imagine the devastation that could result if they did *not* stay in perfect formation. That gives us another sobering reason to work together—not only for mutual benefit but also to avoid conflict and destruction. I have begun to appreciate that the idea of harmony is manifested in every aspect of existence.

- When disharmony results there's no need to give up. In the movies, when a scene is captured on film it's called a "take." When the scene doesn't turn out well it's called a "mis-take" and they shoot it again until they get it right. (And when the sound doesn't record correctly, they use the process of ADR to fix it!) I wonder why we don't see life that way. We all make mistakes, but why beat up on ourselves or others? Why not just redo it, learn from the mistake and fix it, so that the movie of life comes out all right. If experience means making mistakes, then I have lots of experience.

- A movie that fits into this theme of harmony is *Close Encounters of the Third Kind* (1977, Columbia Pictures, dir. by Steven Spielberg). Richard Dreyfuss plays Roy Neary, who has an encounter with a UFO on a dark road, and afterward finds himself obsessed with a mental image of a mountain in the wilderness. He eventually finds the mountain site, where scientists are attempting to make contact with UFOs. In a climactic scene, the scientists connect with aliens by replaying a distinctive five-note phrase reportedly transmitted by the UFOs. The alien aircraft responds, and together the scientists and the aliens "sing" a duet. What a beautiful scene and a profound metaphor about achieving harmony. The tagline from the movie, "We are not alone," is so true. We are all connected and affect each other, so let us find a way to achieve harmony.

- It's also important for each of us to find internal harmony. If we aren't on the right wavelength within ourselves, we may disconnect internally or externally. This, unfortunately, happens all the time between couples, friends and co-workers, within families, in neighbourhoods, among nations, and between peoples of all cultures.

● It is often said that mutual problem solving requires good-will on all sides. If there isn't goodwill between the parties there must at least be goodwill towards a jointly accepted outcome. Whenever I sense that goodwill exists between the parties in conflict, I identify it to give encouragement; if goodwill is absent, that too needs to be addressed so everyone can be made aware that it is lacking.

One metaphor that helps explain this theme of harmony is the children's song *Dem Bones, Dem Bones, Dem Dry Bones* (lyrics by James Weldon Johnson). Although the song is not anatomically correct, it is often used to teach children about how the parts of our bodies are connected, so every part affects the whole. Ironically, then, we need to "bone up" on learning how to be in harmony with one anoth-er! Another example is the banyan tree on the island of Maui, Hawaii that has so many trunks that it looks like a small forest. In fact, though, this is one 50-foot tree that has grown 12 subsidiary trunks and now measures more than 200 feet from side to side. All these examples should help us be conscious of how closely connected we are in life, and help us realize that the resolution or non-resolution of any problem will influence and affect others.

# 7 ARE YOU LOOKING IN THE RIGHT PLACE FOR THE SOLUTION?

*Have you looked beneath the surface to find the solution?*

IN 2000, JUST AFTER my wife Mary and I had moved into our new house, our friends Joellene and Roy came from Akwesasne to help us unpack and get settled in. Joellene was the executive director of the mediation centre in Akwesasne and her husband Roy was an accomplished iron worker and homebuilder.

Our friends had kindly offered to help us for a couple of days. Since things were in such disarray, with furniture and boxes everywhere, the only bed available was a sofa bed.

**In desperation I pulled and kicked the couch, all to no avail.**

We were all upstairs one evening when I was asked to go downstairs to open the sofa bed and get it ready for Joellene and Roy.

But after I'd removed the cushions from the couch, I could not open up the bed. Despite considerable pulling and tugging, for the life of me I could not pull the mattress out of the couch. In desperation I pulled and even kicked the couch, all to no avail. I am totally useless when it comes to any kind of manual task, but this one I had done many times before so I was puzzled.

"Ernie, how are you doing with the couch?" Mary called from upstairs.

"Fine," I answered quickly, not wanting to admit that I couldn't do something as elementary as open the sofa bed.

A few minutes later I was still struggling when she called down again: "Ernie, is everything OK? Why aren't you up here by now? Do you need some help?"

No! There was absolutely no way that I was going to ask for help! I didn't want to look inadequate nor admit to anyone that I'd been defeated by a stupid couch!

"No problem, just give me a minute," I lied, trying to buy more time.

Before we'd moved I'd opened the bed many times, so I decided the only explanation was that the moving company had damaged the sofa bed and was to blame for

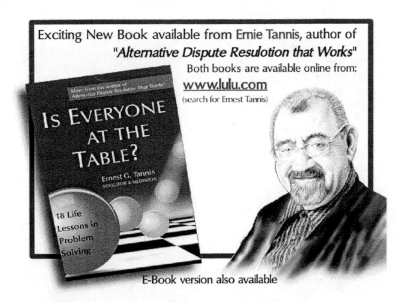
## What Others are Saying about the Book!

"This is a remarkable, highly readable and insightful collection of real-world events that prove the importance of ADR's ability to resolve conflicts, peacefully, in today's world."

John W. McDonald, U.S. Ambassador (ret'd)
Chairman and CEO, Institute for Multi-Track Diplomacy
Author of The Shifting Grounds of Conflict and Peacebuilding: Stories and Lessons

"As a fellow pioneer in the field, I continue to admire your steadfast commitment to social justice and peace, and your never-ending effort to provide people in conflict, and society more broadly, with alternative (and better) ways of resolving disputes and seeking consensus."

Dr. Ben Hoffman, Ph. D.
Author, Peace Guerilla

"I went from laughter to tears and at times to exploring my own journey...I will value this book both in my life and my practice..."

Gord Breedyk
Co-Chair Canadian Civilian Peace Service

"...each story...is filled with emotion, love and wisdom. What a gift!"

Bruce Rosove
Life Coach, Coach Instructor, Consultant,
Emotional Fitness Institute

More....

"...I absolutely loved it... Your book has taught me so much and I plan to use the techniques in my couples counselling session…"

Anita Rizvi
Couples Counsellor

Your new book is very good. ...answers to valuable questions were handled in layman's terms and gave excellent alternatives!!

Jane Burton
Retired Elementary School Teacher

"...This is so easy to read—I can't believe that it is written by a lawyer. The lessons are so very clear and your passion for the topic shine through."

Leota Embleton
Director, Ontario Lawyers Assistance Program

"...Oh you are a beautiful writer, and your writing also teaches so well..."

Helena Cornelius
Core Team: Australian Conflict Resolution Network

my difficulties. But before I could decide what else to try, I heard the words I had been dreading: "Ernie, I'm sending Roy down to help you."

I hated that I needed help with this simple task, but I was comforted knowing that the problems had obviously been caused by someone else. After all, what can be done if it's someone else's fault?

"Need help?" asked Roy as he came down the stairs.

"There's something wrong with the couch and it won't open," I said, trying not to show my frustration. "It probably got damaged in the move."

## I didn't want to admit that I had been defeated by the couch.

Roy tried to pull out the bed just as I had, and when that didn't work he immediately got down on his hands and knees and lifted up a corner of the couch so he could peer underneath.

I immediately felt vindicated since even this very accomplished tradesperson was having trouble. After a few minutes he reached underneath and started manipulating something.

*Aha!* I thought. *So it was broken! I knew it!*

Roy stood up and effortlessly pulled the bed from the couch. I was mystified.

"What did you do?" I asked in bewilderment, amazed and relieved that the problem was fixed, yet dismayed that I had not been able to figure out how to fix it.

"I just figured that the movers must have tied up the spring mechanism to prevent the bed from opening up when they were carrying it," shrugged Roy. "I just had to find where it was tied."

Such a simple answer to what for me had been a complex problem!

I thanked Roy and then we went back upstairs, and in a very kind way Roy explained what had happened. I felt sheepish as Roy told the story, but when the women started laughing I also had to admit that it was quite funny. We all laughed together. "Way to go, Roy," I said.

This is such a simple story but for me it has profound meaning.

## SOME LESSONS

- At times we don't go deep enough to find the source of the problem, and that prevents us from coming up with the right solution. In this story, I kept approaching the problem in the same way, which was the only way I knew, but I never made any progress. However, when I finally allowed someone to assist me, that person looked beyond the obvious, approached the situation from a different angle, and dug a little deeper to find the source of the problem. Once that person found the cause, the solution proved to be simple. In mediation situations often the best way to break a deadlock is to bring in a fresh mind to consider the problem from another angle.

- Many times we feel too foolish or embarrassed to admit we need help and, as I did in this story, we procrastinate as long as possible in asking for assistance because of pride, feelings of inadequacy or shame. But remember that it's impossible for one person to have all the skills and expertise needed to fix every problem. Accept that sometimes it's necessary to seek help from someone who *does* have the right skills, and save yourself the frustration!

- Often we choose to look only on the surface for a solution because we're afraid to look underneath, where the situation might be dark or messy. But every situation and every person has an element of darkness or a hidden side, and as much as we want to avoid that side, that's often exactly where we need to look. This was quite a revelation for me and remains an ongoing struggle. It's important to make sure that we're thorough in finding and settling every issue, since just one unresolved or unaddressed issue can come back to cause more problems. To use a down-to-earth metaphor, just one unresolved issue can become like the burr under the saddle that causes a horse to buck and perhaps throw off the rider.

I had a toothache for a long time, but by the time I visited a dentist a root canal was needed to fix what could have been fixed so simply with a filling. Worse, after the root canal I was supposed to have a crown put on the tooth, but the dentist's office neglected to call me with a follow-up appointment, and ultimately the tooth had to be pulled. This applies to many situations: if you wait too long to ask for help—or if you don't get the right help—the problem can worsen.

There is a second lesson to this story, as only recently have I been able to resolve my anger over the loss of that tooth. For years I blamed the dentist entirely for the missed appointment and the excruciating pain I suffered, which is contrary to my belief that everyone in a problem usually has contributed to the dispute, and therefore must also contribute to the solution. I eventually realized that I had to accept equal responsibility, since I had not followed up with the dentist's office. This realization allowed me to forgive the dentist and myself, move past my anger, and accept this as a lesson learned.

## So it was broken!
### I knew it!

# 8 WHAT DO YOU VALUE?

---

*The only thing to give up on in life is giving up.*

A FEW YEARS AGO, a couple was involved in a hostile family litigation that had been dragging on for more than two years. One of the lawyers brought an application under the *Family Law Act* for the appointment of a mediator, which in itself is a creative negotiation tactic. The two lawyers nominated several mediators, and I was selected.

The two lawyers were present for the first mediation session, but I held the second session alone with the couple. It was obvious that they did not trust each other, especially after such acrimonious and expensive litigation.

## What values do I wish to live by, and are my actions consistent with those values?

The father was deeply depressed over the breakup and the mother's departure from the house with the children and the assets. The mother was also distressed and in fear, and was now living with her parents.

Despite their hostility towards each other, it was important to find their common ground as a basis to start the mediation. I sensed that they both loved their children, and on that they both agreed—in fact, it was the first point on which they could agree. What could I do or say next to encourage the couple to negotiate?

In mediation terminology we were in what is known as the "dark moment" of the mediation when even the mediator is unsure of the next step. The situation was deadlocked and it seemed all channels of communication were broken. I decided the only way to restart the dialogue was to ask a question, although I had no idea what that question would be.

I turned to the woman. "I want to ask you a question," I began. "Is that OK with you?" I still didn't know what I was going to ask her, but I trusted that I'd think of something.

And then the words came to me. "What values do you live by?" I asked. To this day I don't really know what prompted me to ask that particular question.

"I'm a Christian," she said.

The man interrupted and complained that all of that religious stuff was nonsense, and added that the children were being misled. It was a moment of truth.

"What values do you live by?" I asked him.

"People live and die. That's it," he said simply.

Silence.

In litigation training, young lawyers are told, "never ask a question for which you don't know the answer." In mediation, however, I have found the opposite to be true.

So without any idea how the father would respond, I said to him, "How you resolve your conflict will be the only real education your children will have in solving problems in life, so what values would you like your children to have?"

He began listing values and ideals that he would be proud to see in his children. I could hardly keep up with him as I wrote the long list on the flip chart. When the page was full, I pointed to the extensive number of items and asked the couple: "Is that list a common set of values you can both work towards?"

They both agreed it was, and that proved to be enough to nudge the couple to keep working toward a solution. After a few more sessions the couple went their separate ways, got a divorce, and completed the ADR process. They felt a duty, if not to each other then at least to their children. They always negotiated in good faith and resolved their differences by going back to those values. At the end they felt they had approached a sense of justice for themselves and their children.

Values help us to form an important foundation in life, yet I've come to realize that we tend to take a backward approach in our society. We're so concerned about our "rights" that we tend to push discussions about values to the back burner. As this story shows, focusing on "rights" and other legal issues gets us nowhere. Instead, I propose we begin by asking ourselves: "What values do I wish to

live by and are my actions consistent with those values?" When we begin with that perspective, it's amazing how differently a problem can be understood and possibly resolved. Let me provide another vivid example of this principle at work:

Two businessmen were in conflict over an issue related to whether a commission was payable on a commercial real estate leasing transaction. At stake was $100,000, which was a substantial amount of money at the time. At their request, I began talking to them informally about a process I had begun pursuing, which was pre-litigation mediation, or mediation before any court action is taken. I figured that in appropriate cases this would be a natural next step in cost-effective and mutually respectful problem solving.

Both parties had already spoken to their lawyers about commencing a lawsuit so I spoke with both lawyers, who were understandably concerned about what impact this unfamiliar procedure would have on any future litigation. Everyone felt litigation was inevitable since the dispute seemed to come down to a win-lose (zero-sum game) outcome—either the whole $100,000 was owed or none of it was.

**They resolved their differences by going back to those values.**

I wrote up a pre-litigation mediation agreement for everyone to consider, which was quite novel at the time. According to the ground rules we established, we agreed to a mutual fact-finding and law-finding mediation approach. As a lawyer I would do the legal research, and as a mediator I would give out legal information but not legal advice. The entire mediation process would be without prejudice, so nothing said or done could be used in court proceedings, but if no settlement resulted and litigation commenced—a claim and a counterclaim—it was expected that this joint first step would substantially reduce the cost for the pleadings, examinations for discovery and trial, if it went that far.

There was pressure around those two businesspeople from their associates, families and friends on how to deal with the circumstance. That is not unlike any dispute, when everyone around you has an opinion, so there is a tendency to appease many other interests and points of view before making a decision.

Each party had been told by his lawyer that it would cost $25,000 to commence the court action and take it through all the procedural steps before trial, and it would cost *another* $25,000 for the trial itself. In other words, for the $100,000 at stake, each party was prepared to spend $50,000 for a win-or-lose outcome, knowing that the "winner" could also be ordered to pay to the "loser" substantial legal costs. Of course, after the trial there would always be the possibility that one of the parties would appeal the judge's decision, leading to even more legal costs and time delays.

In contrast to the very costly trial option, for the pre-litigation mediation we agreed to a fee of only $5,000, or $2,500 each. This relatively low sum would also save on future legal costs if there were no settlement, since so much legal research would already be done.

Both court lawyers, the barristers, agreed to this process but no one really felt a solution was possible. After a few weeks my report was done but, alas, despite their best efforts in the mediation they could not find any middle ground. Both parties thanked me for my attempt, and neither felt the mediation exercise had been a waste of time or money, although many around them had hoped to avoid a public conflict between these well-known and highly regarded businessmen. The court lawyers expressed gratitude for what they termed the "failed effort" but in reality they were probably grateful they could finally get on with the litigation. I recollect that this happened on a Thursday and that the litigation was set to begin the following Monday.

After they left my office I spent some time reflecting about the "failed effort" and I recalled the line from Rudyard Kipling's poem *If*, "If you can meet with triumph and disaster and treat those two imposters just the same..." From the beginning of my ADR journey I had determined that in mediation it's impossible to think in terms of "triumph" (success) or "disaster" (failure), because it's impossible to know what will result from the mediation over time. I've had many tough experiences that verify that. As I was mulling over the situation, it occurred to me that although we had looked at the law, I had neglected to ask one vital question.

I called the first gentleman and asked if I could see him briefly that afternoon. He questioned whether another meeting would make any difference, but when I told him I needed to ask him an important question, he kindly consented.

"I'm very curious to know what question you feel you need to ask," he said when I met him a short time later in his boardroom.

"My question is this: What value system do you live by? What informs your decision making in your personal and business life? And do you believe you are applying that value system to this situation?"

He excused himself for a few minutes and returned with a text from the Torah, the sacred scriptures of Judaism. He read the words in Hebrew from Deuteronomy 16:20 and explained that he interpreted the meaning as "righteousness, righteousness."

When I asked him what that meant, he replied, "Well, Ernie, it essentially means that whatever I do must be righteous not only for me but also for those in the community."

"Can community include the other person you are in dispute with, and in our own community?" I asked.

"Of course," he replied.

So I continued: "Do you think that the decision to proceed to litigation fits both levels of righteousness?"

"I don't know," he replied. "I haven't thought about it that way. Let me think about it and I'll get back to you."

I was appreciative and told him I was planning to call the other party and ask the same question.

When I called the other gentleman and explained what

had just transpired, even before I could ask my question he said, "We Christians have our own value system too. I can go to the Bible and read what Jesus taught." He later called back and said he had just read the exhortation in Philippians 2:4 to look out not only for your own interests, but also for the interests of others.

I went home comforted that there was still some thinking going on. As the saying goes, if they're talking, at least they're not fighting. I had no idea what the outcome would be, but as a neutral intervener I'd learned to have "a sincere indifference to the outcome." In my heart I secretly hoped something would come **I had done all I could and the next move was up to them.** of this last attempt but I had to remind myself that I had done all I could and the next move was up to them.

The next day, to my pleasant surprise, I heard back from both parties. Each called to say he was prepared to resume our discussion that day to see if litigation could be avoided. However, this was now Friday, and with litigation set to begin the following Monday we were down to the wire.

The details of the final discussion aren't important nor do I even remember them. What I do remember is that before sunset that Friday, before the beginning of the Jewish Sabbath, they were successful in reaching an agreement, which they signed.

I commended both of them for doing something spectacular, not only for themselves but also for the mediation process, by introducing values as a core part of the dialogue.

If you're wondering, that Friday afternoon I did speak with both lawyers, who had to review the agreement to ensure both parties obtained independent legal advice before signing. Both lawyers said they were pleased for their respective clients, but knowing how much money those lawyers would have earned through litigation, I wondered how they really felt!

## SOME LESSONS

● Whenever you have reached an impasse, try to see the situation from a different angle. A deadlock doesn't have to mean a dead end. To break the deadlock, step back from the issues and see how your own values or sense of purpose in life can help move past the impasse.

● No matter how many bumps you encounter on the road to a solution or reconciliation, keep going and don't be afraid to try a different route. Remember that when you use a GPS it offers alternative routes and will recalculate your route if you turn a different way; to reach a solution or a reconciliation you may need to adopt that same GPS approach. To find the best route to your destination, let your values or the principles that you believe in guide your way to help get past any confusion, doubts, or fears.

● Get involved in resolving others' issues only if you are invited, and once invited, keep going until you are asked to stop, even if the disputants stop moving. Try giving them a nudge. Make sure the values you bring to the table are not compromised.

● Whatever you are doing, saying or thinking, check yourself out to see if it resonates with your values. I heard about a delivery boy who called his supervisor, pretending he was a potential customer, and asked if the delivery person was reliable. When asked why, he said "I wanted to check up on myself." One of the guests on my ADR radio show told me about an exercise in which you pick three core values that describe your life, and then measure all that you do against them.

# 9 WHO OR WHAT DO YOU TRUST?

*If not now, then when?*
*If not here, then where?*
*If not this, then what?*

WHEN MY DAUGHTER Chanda was a young girl of about five, we went for a walk on Victoria Island in Ottawa, which is named for Queen Victoria and is part of the original Algonquin national lands here in Canada's capital.

On arriving, I parked my car near a wall and we walked around the park for some time, and eventually started making our way back. At some point on the other side of the park Chanda stepped onto the beginning of the stone wall and started walking along the top. We kept talking as we ambled back and I didn't notice how quickly the wall had increased in height, nor the growing distance between us. By the time we reached the parking lot I was surprised to look up from the ground level to see my young daughter standing on the top of a six-foot wall.

> I decided it would be much quicker if she jumped down from the wall.

The car was parked just next to me, and I quickly calculated how long it would take Chanda to walk back down the wall to the beginning and

# "No, Daddy!
## It's too far to jump!"

return to the car. I decided it would be quicker if she simply jumped down from the wall, and I also thought jumping might be fun for her.

"Chanda, please jump down so we can go to the car
now," I said, looking up at her.

"No, Daddy! It's too far to jump!"

Suddenly I became aware that for a small child of her
age, the thought of jumping from that height was not fun
at all, but in fact was quite frightening. I saw fear in her
young face, and instantly I felt that parental urge to take
away my child's fear and provide reassurance.

"Don't worry, 3D, I promise I'll catch you," I said. 3D
was the nickname I'd coined for her, which was short for
Dad's Darling Daughter. "Please jump."

I stretched out my arms to show her how I would
catch her.

She began crying. "But Daddy, I'm scared!"

For some reason that became a moment of truth for me. My first priority was, of course, to make sure she was safe and unharmed. But it was also a teachable moment for both of us about how we approach life's risks and how we need to trust one another.

"Come on, Chanda. I promise I'll catch you. Just jump down. It's not that far."

This was becoming an increasingly emotional situation for both of us, but I was determined to carry through with it.

Once more I pleaded with her. "Please, Chanda. Trust your father. Please jump."

I could see tears well up in her eyes and I knew that for a young child, choosing to trust in a situation like this had to be a difficult. I also understood that this was about how I was learning to take a leap of faith in life, and how important it was to me that she make that jump.

I had a feeling that this moment mirrored my own questions about faith and about the importance of moving forward in life toward whatever one believes in. Many times I'd had to remind myself how important it is to get past the fear and take a step forward, even if it feels uncertain. It's difficult to trust in something you can't see, but that's what faith is.

As I waited for Chanda to decide, there was no pressure, but rather a sense of presence. No more words were exchanged; I recall just looking at Chanda and trying to reassure her through my eyes. As I write this, the experience is as vivid now as it was then.

She took a step off the wall and jumped. I can see in my mind's eye my beautiful little girl in midair falling towards me, totally trusting that she would be OK. What an act of courage. I don't recall anything at that moment; only that my entire focus was on catching her and making sure she was safe.

She landed safely in my arms and I squeezed her as tightly as I could. We stood there for a moment, fiercely holding onto each other and crying.

"Thank you, Chanda," I said.

I have told this story many times over the years, in training sessions and in mediations. Even after all these years I can remember every detail of it, as it was an experience that helped crystallize my philosophy about taking a leap of faith and, in more ways than I could have imagined, has helped guide my life.

## I was also learning to take a leap of faith in life.

I think back long ago when I was following my heart in beginning this ADR journey. I had left a lucrative law practice and this new path had caused much financial and emotional stress on my family. One night my son, Derek, then a young teenager, said, "No matter what, Dad, what you are doing is untouchable." (I also remember Chanda asking, "Dad, why can't you follow your heart *after* you make your money back?") I thank my two children for their trust in what I was doing.

When I eventually became immersed in third-party neutral intervention, I was involved in a mediation situation with a major corporation in which there was deep mistrust among various stakeholders. I spoke with the senior executive about trust and told him this story about Chanda, and ended with the oft-quoted adage, "Love many, trust few, but always paddle your own canoe." In response, he said he didn't trust anyone; in fact, he didn't even trust himself. I realized then how important it is to begin by trusting yourself, and talking to him made me think back to times when I also lost faith in myself or in God—or I felt that others and God had lost faith in me. But I never lost faith in my faith. I suggested to this man that he use trust as a bridge to hope.

Every day we all choose to trust as part of our daily lives. Look at how much we trust, for example, that traffic lights, elevators, transportation systems, and all sorts of computerized systems will work as they're supposed to, and how much faith we put in professional advisors, friends and even strangers.

What is the most devastating experience in the world? I think it's when mistrust enters a relationship. In marriage, infidelity is a breach of trust that can destroy the relationship at its most profound level. History is full of stories of people who have been betrayed, taken advantage of, bilked of their life savings or violently abused by those they trusted. All the more reason to ask, how can one take a leap of faith in such a world? I learned from a Mohawk counsellor named Harry that life is like a battery; there's both a negative and a positive side, and you need both so that the engine of life can drive you forward.

## SOME LESSONS

- Don't leave yourself stranded in life. Choose to trust someone or something. If you ever were stuck in the snow, who would you call so that you didn't feel helpless or freeze to death?

- Always keep a toolkit—like a multi-function Swiss Army knife—in your mind for dealing with various situations. Trust is like a knife that opens up umpteen options to deal with many situations.

- As part of my ADR journey, I have learned to say to disputants in mediations: Do not let your mistrust keep you from the dialogue; bring your feelings of mistrust to the table as part of the discussion.

- We all have different perspectives that determine how we respond to situations. To me, an adult, the wall that Chanda was walking along didn't seem that high and the jump didn't appear that dangerous; to her, a young child, the wall probably seemed impossibly high and the jump incredibly dangerous.

- Leaps of faith are a big part of life, consciously or unconsciously. One of my favourite movie scenes occurs near the end of *Indiana Jones and the Last Crusade* (1989, Paramount Pictures, dir. by Steven Spielberg), when Indiana Jones (Harrison Ford) stands at the edge of a dark abyss with no way to get across to the other side. He takes a deep breath and extends one foot out into the seemingly empty space. Just as we think he's going to fall into the empty blackness, out of nowhere a foot bridge appears and allows him to cross. When I described this scene to a friend, I said, "His leap of faith made that bridge appear." My friend responded, "The bridge was always there, but he didn't know it until he took a step forward."

# 10 DID YOU THINK IT THROUGH BEFORE FORMING AN OPINION?

*Each ripple can become a wave to wash away unresolved conflict from the shores of injustice.*[1]

IN THE MID-1990S, a husband who had heard about my approaches in mediation and ADR asked me to settle a family law dispute between him and his wife. Both parties wanted a fair and respectful solution that would avoid a long, costly, adversarial divorce proceeding, but there was a lot of mistrust.

After hearing the facts as the husband related them to me, as his solicitor I suggested a without prejudice pre-litigation four-way negotiation, a technique I had learned from my colleague Evita Roach. I explained to my client that the purpose and value of this negotiation technique is to encourage the parties to listen to each other before litigation. I

**Professional advisors are obliged, legally and ethically, to learn about all the options.**

---

1  These words came to me at an ADR conference in the U.S. Near the end of the conference I sent up a note to the chairperson, Chief Justice Frank Evans of the Texas Court of Appeals. To my surprise, he used my words in his closing speech, and thereafter he and I interacted for years. In fact, he endorsed my first book in 1989 and was a guest on the ADR show on CHIN radio in Ottawa. He is among those who have truly advanced ADR in North America, and he very much encouraged my own path.

had effectively used this technique with lawyers who had initially been reluctant.

My client had never heard of the approach but liked the sound of it. He understood that without prejudice meant that nothing said or done during the procedure could be used in a court or any legal proceeding so it would be a safe, structured setting for everyone to express themselves openly. Skilled, experienced people would facilitate, and after both parties had received independent legal advice, only the final binding agreement would be admissible and enforceable in a court of law.

## The word voodoo suggested that ADR was some sort of cult or superstitious belief.

With the husband's consent I then contacted the lawyer acting for the wife. John Webster was a prominent and very accomplished family law barrister, or a court-room lawyer, whom I had known and respected for many years. John had developed a reputation as a very aggressive and accomplished litigator with a focus on family law. He liked the thrust and parry of the win-lose adversarial process. I knew that to convince him to engage in this four-way pre-litigation negotiation procedure would be a challenge. On top of that, I had to make sure John knew that I was no longer a barrister, having left trial work several years previously to focus on my practice as a solicitor, or a lawyer that attends to legal matters outside the courtroom. That was important for John to know because if this case could not be settled and ended up in court, I would not act as the court lawyer although I would stay on as a negotiating solicitor.

When I suggested the four-way negotiation approach to John, he said he'd never heard of it before, which did not surprise me. But I *was* very surprised by his response: "Ernie, I have been following your contributions on ADR, and while I admire you for your efforts in negotiation and settlement options, I will not be part of your voodoo ADR!"

I was stunned. I'd experienced many objections to ADR before but John's use of the word voodoo suggested that ADR was some sort of cult or superstitious belief not to be taken seriously. It reminded me of an experience I'd had with one of the lawyers in a business dispute. At the request of the other side, I'd suggested the dispute be resolved through mediation. This lawyer, however, refused to talk to me and instead sent me a profanity-laced message leaving no doubt how he felt about ADR. But after I talked with him, he changed his mind and a settlement was reached that saved the business.

After John's rebuke, I took a moment to decide how to respond. Finally I came up with an analogy I thought he would appreciate, and I said, "John, you're an established court lawyer. If a witness took the stand in court and under oath repeated what someone had told them, would you say anything to the judge?"

"Of course I would object to the judge," he said immediately, "and challenge that such evidence is hearsay and not admissible, since I would need the right to directly cross-examine the person who had said anything to the witness on the stand."

"OK, John, then what evidence do you have that indicates this four-way pre-litigation negotiation is not useful?"

"Well, honestly, I haven't experienced such a process."

I then shared with him another experience I'd had years earlier. In that case I was acting for the wife, and the husband's lawyer had told his client that the mediation technique I had suggested was inappropriate to resolve their family law issues. I described to John the three questions I'd asked that lawyer:

"From the theories and principles of mediation found in the literature, which of those theories and principles do not apply to this case?" The other lawyer said he had not read any such literature.

"From all the training and educational programs you have attended in conflict resolution, mediation and ADR, what tells you that this case cannot benefit from mediation?" The lawyer said he had not attended any such training.

## I was confident John would tell others about the benefit of this negotiation option.

"From from all your experiences in third-party neutral interventions, what tells you that this assisted negotiation approach to mediation will not work for this couple?" The lawyer replied that he did not have much experience with those processes.

So I suggested to that lawyer that when the lives of people are at stake, professional advisors—in all disciplines—are obliged, legally and ethically, to learn about all the options available to their clients even if they disagree with them, rather than just saying no.

When I had finished telling John this story, he sat for a moment then finally said, "OK, Ernie, I'll go through with this process you suggested and see for myself. I don't expect I'll feel any different afterward, but you're right. I'll give it a try."

We then embarked on the four-way pre-litigation process as I'd suggested. John and I began by working together to jointly craft an agenda for the session, which in itself is a huge step in making sure a meeting is productive. Too often people go into meetings to solve problems without any process guidelines, which can make things worse. By the time we had created the joint document John was beginning to open up and even commented that he thought things were already starting to move along.

After a three-hour session the couple arrived at a settlement, much to the surprise of John and his client, the wife. He and I agreed to leave and prepare an agreement for the couple to sign.

Afterward, John came to talk to me privately. "I have to admit that I'm pleasantly surprised, Ernie. I've never before seen anything like this four-way process, but I'm sold. Thanks for encouraging me to try it."

"And thank you, John, for being willing to try it," I replied. "Your participation and support for these ADR options will certainly have a positive impact in our community." I was confident that John would tell other colleagues and clients about the benefit of this negotiation option, and was sure his influence in the legal community would carry a lot of weight.

My client, the husband, was also pleased with how the process had worked. However, because he didn't trust his wife he felt uncomfortable about the agreement. The next day I received a letter asking me to transfer the file to another lawyer, and I never heard from the client again.

About a year later I was conducting another separation and divorce mediation, and this time both spouses were my joint clients. At my request John helped out by doing something that at the time was not very common. He came in as a neutral third party and openly gave the couple legal information, not legal advice, about the strengths and weaknesses of their respective situations on the same set of facts. This allowed the couple to find out what guidance and legal information each of them might receive if they were to seek independent legal advice from two separate lawyers. John said he was pleased to participate in this unique approach, and the couple was satisfied that they did not need to go to separate lawyers and try to outdo each other legally. The case turned out very well;

in fact, it was written up in a column in the *Ottawa Citizen* as an example of non-adversarial conflict resolution.

Afterward I asked John if he knew what had happened to the couple involved in the four-way negotiation the previous year. All that John knew was that both parties had run out of money and represented themselves after that. *More damage done that could have been avoided*, I thought to myself. I still wonder to this day whatever became of that couple and their family.

A few years ago John Webster died. At his funeral, I told this story to some of his family members and mentioned how much I had respected John's open-mindedness and courage in helping introduce these ADR options to people. I told them how his attitude had inspired and encouraged me, and asked his family if I could honour his memory by telling this story and crediting him with contributing to the development of ADR in our community. They said they would be pleased to have his memory honoured in this way, and now I have finally been able to do it.

> I respected John's open-mindedness and courage in helping introduce ADR options.

Thank you, John, and may your memory be eternal.

## SOME LESSONS

- When you hear a no, don't let that deter you. Instead, take that as an opportunity to enjoy a different discussion from what you had planned. Ask that person why they are saying no so that you can better understand that person's point of view and see if a common ground can be found or obstacles overcome. When we meet resistance, too often we get into discussions about right and wrong rather than actively listening to all sides of the issue.

- Don't automatically defend or counter every comment made. Ask questions and share your values or belief system to encourage others to rethink their positions. Try to get to the underlying issues so that the outcome is mutual and fair. My colleague Tom Colosi once said that the goal of an effective negotiation is not to convince the other person of your point of view but rather to create doubt in that person's mind of his or her own point of view.

- Be confident in yourself; don't worry about rumours and accusations. Stand firm in your belief in yourself and what you are doing, as long as there is goodwill between all parties.

- Be grateful to those who listen and are willing to change. Acknowledge that positive development as an accomplishment in itself.

- As the subtitle to this chapter says, remember that even small changes can cumulatively add up to a big movement, so don't be discouraged if your initiatives seem small. I learned this from the late Gordon Henderson, a well-respected senior partner of an Ottawa law firm who wrote the foreword to my 1989 book. Gordon once asked me how the developments in ADR had begun, and when I shared my experiences, he simply said, "Oh, I see. One thing leads to another." When you follow your heart you never know where it will lead you. So, be a ripple. To me, John was such a ripple.

# 11 DO YOU FOLLOW YOUR OWN PRINCIPLES?

*Point the way, not a finger.*

TWO COLLEAGUES and I met on a Saturday morning at a very popular breakfast restaurant to prepare for a week-long training session in mediation. This was our only opportunity to meet before the training that was to begin on Monday, and we knew we had at least a few hours of work ahead of us.

We arrived at the restaurant early, knowing how hard it would be to get a booth on a weekend, so we were delighted when we were seated in a large booth with a table large enough for our breakfast and all the papers we needed.

## The lineup snaked out the door and down the sidewalk.

When we finished our breakfast, the waiter cleared away our dishes, refilled our coffee and brought our bill, and we spread out our papers, binders, and schedules all across the table and settled into our work session. A few minutes later the waiter returned to ask if we would pay the bill. We thought that was odd since we clearly weren't leaving anytime soon, but we gave him a credit card and added a generous tip when he came back with the receipt.

I had assumed that we could continue working without any further interruption, but the waiter just stood by the table, clearly wanting something. The three of us looked at him, bewildered.

"Can I help you?" I asked. We had been here many times before, and I recognized the waiter as the owner's son.

He pointed to the front door of the restaurant. "Look at that lineup of people waiting to come into the restaurant."

The three of us turned and I saw that the lineup snaked out the door and down the sidewalk, which only made me thankful that we had arrived early and secured this large booth.

"OK, I see," I said. "But why are you telling us that? We know you're always busy, and that's why we came early."

"You are finished your breakfast and have paid your bill, so normally you would leave soon," said the waiter. "But you look like you intend to stay a long while, and that means this booth will not be available for more customers who would buy more breakfasts. So by staying here you are making us lose business."

I couldn't recall ever being asked to leave a restaurant to make room for others, and my first reaction was that as paying customers we had the right to stay. There was no rule that said we were required to leave even when the restaurant was busy.

Ironically, the training that my colleagues and I were planning that day was based on "principled negotiation," in which the mediator encourages the disputants to get beyond their respective positions to find out each other's underlying interests, and then brainstorm options for mutual gain.

I was much too focused on our work to think about applying the principles.

But at the time I was not considering any of these mediation principles; I was totally set on accomplishing my own objective, which was to finish what we were working on.

"But you know we're good customers and we come here often," I protested. "Just look at everything we've spread out over the table. This is the only opportunity we have to meet so we can't leave until we finish our work."

I was afraid of what might result if my colleagues and I had to disband. We still had work to do, there was no other time we could meet, and we were expecting 20 participants on Monday morning. At some level I knew the conscientious thing to do was to stop thinking about our "rights," vacate the booth and find another place to meet. I could appreciate that the restaurant didn't want to lose business, and they couldn't afford to have us occupy a table while so many other customers stood in line waiting. I reasoned, however, that on this particular day we needed to continue working exactly where we were since we didn't have time to pack up, move to another location and restart our work session.

I realized we were deadlocked. There was no hostility between us; however, the problem looked too difficult to resolve so that both sides could gain. Contrary to the win-

win philosophy of the mediation training that we were there to plan, it seemed we were facing a win-lose outcome. I sensed that we all wanted a friendly, mutually beneficial outcome, but what would that outcome be?

"Is there anything we can do to settle this so that both of us benefit?" asked one of my colleagues. This principle is essential to ADR, but I must admit that even though I was the lead trainer for the upcoming session I was much too focused on the work ahead to think about applying that principle.

## By applying the principles of our training to the situation, Bob found a solution.

At that point my other colleague, Bob, jumped in. "We really should be able to stay here," he said to the waiter, "but what will you lose if we do that? We don't want you to lose anything." I realized that Bob had just referred to the ADR principles the three of us would be teaching on Monday morning.

"We would lose the sale of at least three more breakfasts since this booth holds four people," said the waiter.

"Plus, you would lose another tip, right?" Bob added.

The waiter nodded.

Bob continued, "OK, so your main interest is to not lose another round of breakfast sales or another tip, and our interest is to stay and complete our work since we don't have any other practical alternative."

That seemed to properly sum up each of our underlying interests, a principle that was at the heart of our upcoming training session. I waited, fascinated, to hear what would come next.

"So," Bob continued, "why don't we just pay you for another round of breakfast plus a tip? You won't have to serve us any more food, and we can stay and finish our work. Both of us will get what we want. Would that be an acceptable solution?"

At that point I had one of those moments that the

dean of my law school would have called "an illuminating glimpse of the obvious." By applying the main principles of our upcoming training to our situation Bob had found a solution. During the training sessions, whenever this kind of unexpected issue arose or a conflict presented itself I would use it as a "teach piece," which is exactly what Bob was doing. I only wish I had thought of it! We waited for the waiter's reaction.

The waiter smiled. "Yes, that would be fine. I don't want to cause you any trouble either. If you pay the same amount as you have just paid, including the tip, then you can stay as long as you like and finish your work." Finally an acceptable solution had been found.

So he rang up another bill for exactly the same amount, and we gladly paid it and added exactly the same tip. The waiter was happy since he made a tip and the restaurant made money without having to provide any more food—just unlimited coffee refills. We were happy, too, since we were able to stay and finalize our preparations.

All of us laughed, and I remarked that this experience would be a good story for the training—which it has been, many times.

## SOME LESSONS

- When you're in a real-life conflict situation, it's often difficult to apply your own teachings—it's somewhat like the shoemaker whose children have no shoes. It's easier to tell someone else that they aren't following their own principles than to apply that thinking to yourself. But we'll earn more respect from others if we respect our own values.

- How does one "walk the talk" or "walk the walk and not just talk the walk"? I remember playing football in high school when the defensive captain was telling us how to do a blocking manoeuvre. When I asked him to show us, he did, and by watching his actions the players understood the manoeuvre much more quickly. It reminded me that example is the best education.

● This story reminds us of how we can at times get caught up in a situation to the point that we forget what we stand for. Various influences on us can and do affect how we perceive things. A study was done on a group of people who were gathered in a room to watch a film of two cars involved in an accident. After viewing the film they were told the accident had led to a lawsuit, and were randomly divided into two groups of "eye-witnesses," one for the plaintiff in the case and the other for the defendant. In preparation for the "trial" both groups were extensively questioned about what they'd seen. By the time the trial was held, the two groups had been so influenced by the pre-trial preparation that they had different versions of the same event.

I try to remember this story when I'm seeking to see another person's point of view so that I can be aware of what influences may be affecting my own view-point. As a mediator it's critical to stay neutral and not be influenced by a dispute, and one way to do that is to focus on the mediation process and facilitate the parties to focus on the issues and each other's underlying interest.

● I like to use the metaphor of restaurant menus when we talk about problem solving options, since we have various choices from which to choose, depending on the circumstances and our individual tastes. Consumers have choices and options for every other area of life, why not for conflict resolution as well?

● This is the kind of story that could have had a different outcome had different people been involved. If other people had felt they had a right to stay, they perhaps could have protested and insisted on staying, left in a huff threatening not to return, asked to speak to the manager or offered less compensation to remain in the booth. For me, however, there were many considerations: an existing relationship with the owner, future community connections, and my sensitivity to the financial demands of a small business. All of these factored into the negotiations. For the waiter there were other things to consider: the underlying assumption that the customer has a right to occupy space, and the risk that he could offend the customers.

This simple story reflects the complexities and options inherent in any situation, depending on who is affected, the circumstances, and the attitude and mood of the individuals involved. It also demonstrates how a group needs to work out things themselves to speak with one voice.

# 12 HOW MANY SIDES ARE THERE TO A STORY?

*No matter who you are or think you are, no one ever really knows the whole story.*

IN MY FIRST SEVEN YEARS of practising law, before I chose to become a mediator, I engaged in much litigation, both civil and criminal. Every case was fascinating, if adversarial, and every trial involved the flare and frustration of the courtroom drama.

Trials are so very serious and solemn, and involve many rules, procedures and professional protocols, such as the wearing of court gowns and, of course, the central aspect of deference to the judge. For obvious reasons, a lawyer never wants to upset a judge. To a client involved in litigation nothing is more frightening than seeing the judge rebuke your lawyer, but believe me, it happens. The lawyers on both sides of the case are negotiating with the judge the whole time in marshalling the evidence, examining the witnesses and making submissions at the end of the trial.

**"Your Honour, I see your sign says there are three sides to every story."**

Before the actual trial is the pre-trial conference, or settlement conference, which is the last official attempt to resolve the issues and avoid a trial. The judges at these settlement conferences want to see cases settled and, more often than not, they are. The pre-trial is the first time that the lawyers appear before a judge, but by this time in a case there has already been much legal wrangling: court pleadings, court motions, examinations for discovery with transcripts, many unsuccessful attempts to settle, hostilities, high legal costs, and lots of anxiety on all sides. While the rules of professional conduct require the lawyers on each side to seek a settlement, at the same time they must also be vigorous advocates for their clients. (This schizophrenia is one factor that led me to leave trial work and focus on being a solicitor; I now leave the court work to the barristers and instead handle legal matters outside the courtroom.)

Less than five percent of litigation cases end in a trial, but that small percentage still overloads the legal system. I always remind clients of that fact and ask what makes them think their case is in that five percent. The odds are that their case will be settled, so why not settle earlier rather than later? For one thing, in a negotiation or mediation, the "facts" are what the parties decide them to be, so there is much more flexibility to the settlement when the parties themselves decide what the story is. At a trial or arbitration hearing, however, the judge or arbitrator is the decision maker and the "Trier of Fact," so the judge or arbitrator will determine the facts of the case after hearing all the evidence. I have heard that 80 percent of court and arbitration decisions are based on which side of the story is considered the most credible.

Trials are very risky win-lose propositions. No one can predict the outcome since so many unpredictable factors are at play: how witnesses will do under cross examination, the different views of different judges, how the lawyers do, and a myriad of other influences. Every trial has the inherent danger that the losing side will pay not only their own legal costs but also those of other side. The philosopher Voltaire once wrote: "I never was ruined but twice—once when I lost a lawsuit, and once when I gained one."

The pre-trial is an informal proceeding that is usually held in the judge's chambers or in a courtroom without a court reporter. Lawyers wear business suits rather than court gowns, and their clients—the plaintiff and the defendant—are also present. The judge emphasizes that this settlement conference is without prejudice (meaning that nothing said or done during the pre-trial can be used in a court or any legal proceeding), and that should the case go to trial, a different judge will preside. The judge explains that after hearing all the evidence he or

# I realized I was
## heading down a potentially slippery slope.

she will render a non-binding opinion or prediction as to what might happen at trial if a judgement has to be made. Of course not all such guesses are accurate; in fact, in one of my cases—in which the other side was represented by three lawyers—the pre-trial judge made a recommendation against my client. At trial, however, we won completely with costs, thus demonstrating that these pre-trial predictions must be considered guesses only. Lawyers keep track of their pre-trial experiences with particular judges and the accuracy of their predictions, and all this affects lawyers' decisions on whether to seek a negotiated solution during the pre-trial.

In one such pre-trial, I was pleased to see the judge was someone I very much respected for his fairness. He also happened to be a former mayor of Ottawa. On his wall hung a sign with an old adage I knew well: "There are three sides to every story: yours, mine, and the facts!"

After the judge made his opening comments, I decided I would have some fun and lighten up the situation. The lawyers in a pre-trial tend to put on a kind of show for their clients to exhibit their advocacy skills and diplomatic talents, and to demonstrate how much confidence they have in their cases.

When it was my turn to speak, I said lightly, "Your Honour, I see your sign says that there are three sides to every story, but I have learned over time that, in fact, there is a fourth side to every story."

I expected that the judge would answer me in an equally light-hearted way and ask me about the fourth side. To my great surprise, however, the judge leaned forward and scowled at me. "Pray tell, Mr. Tannis, what is the fourth side to every story?"

I then realized that I was heading down a potentially slippery slope. As I gathered my thoughts I noticed that the other lawyer, his clients, my clients and the judge were all looking at me, waiting for an answer. Have you ever started down a path you were sorry you had chosen but had no way back? Well, that's exactly how I felt.

"Yes, Your Honour, there are four sides to every story." I paused, and I could feel the apprehension in the room, especially from my own clients. "Your side, my side, the facts and then...," I paused again and smiled, hoping my delivery would be perceived as a compliment, "how the judge sees it!"

I figured I had handled it well and avoided a disaster, and I hoped we could now get off this path I'd unintentionally started down. Imagine my horror when the judge, in the tense silence of the chambers, leaned so far forward that his head was nearly resting on his arms and bellowed: "Are you suggesting, Mr. Tannis, that the judge sees anything other than the facts?"

I had an awful sense that this pre-trial was going down the drain, and I noticed my clients shifting uncomfortably in their seats, undoubtedly wondering what I was doing to their case. Meanwhile, the other lawyer was clearly enjoying watching me squirm, and his clients looked relieved that it wasn't their lawyer in the hot seat.

> Meanwhile, the other lawyer was clearly enjoying watching me squirm.

I reminded myself that this was a very fair judge, and I wasn't exactly sure if he was really angry or just putting me on. After a long silence, I became aware that everyone was still waiting for me to respond, so I muttered a quiet prayer for help and forged ahead.

"Well, Your Honour, you see, there are actually *five* sides to every story." I had no idea what the fifth side was, but I was buying time, hoping something clever would come to me so I could pry myself out of this tight spot.

The judge then leaned back in his chair, nodding like he was thinking, and intoned in a slow, determined voice, "Indeed, Mr. Tannis. Five sides to every story, are there? And what, pray tell, would that fifth side be?"

I still wasn't sure what the answer would be, but I had to go for it. The other lawyer was in a state of glee, my clients were clearly horrified, and the other parties were sitting back and enjoying themselves.

"Yes, Your Honour," I began, hoping I'd figure out what to say. "There are five sides to every story, and they are: your side, my side, the facts, how the judge sees it, and the fifth side…," I paused for dramatic effect, feeling the weight of expectation fill the judge's chambers. "The fifth and final side to every story, Your Honour, is of course the truth, which is in every person's heart and soul and ultimately known only to God!" I don't really know where this answer came from, but I feel now that it's something that must have been building in me as a result of many experiences.

I kind of liked what came out and I felt quite relieved to have made a quick recovery. I still didn't know how the judge would react, but I figured it couldn't get any worse.

The judge chuckled, and the sound of his laughter was like beautiful music. "Good comeback, Mr. Tannis," he said good-naturedly. "Now, let's get on with this pre-trial."

Everyone laughed, although probably in different ways. My clients were perceptibly relieved and I'd like to think that my colleague, deep down inside, was also pleased for me. We then went on with the pre-trial and, with the judge's help, settled.

> The judge chuckled, and the sound of his laughter was like beautiful music.

The judge passed away long ago, but I fondly remember him as a very fine judge whose competence was matched by his compassion, his forcefulness and his fairness. I learned quite a lot that day and am grateful for the experience.

## SOME LESSONS

● How often do we form an opinion or make an immediate judgement without knowing the other side of the story? All day, every day, we are bombarded by information from all sides—from 24-hour news channels, the internet, email, and other technology-driven sources. Isn't there a tendency just to go along with what we hear or read because it's easier? Perhaps a wiser approach would be to adopt a healthy scepticism about most of the information we hear or read. If we don't swallow everything we hear, maybe we can avoid intellectual and emotional indigestion. Before accepting what you hear as the truth, remember to ask: How many sides are there to this story?

- Although you think you know the whole story, think of the version you know as just one piece. I remember a playwright telling me a story about the "star of truth" that burst in the heavens. Innumerable pieces of that star fell all over the earth, and each person that picked up a piece ran around saying, "I hold the truth." All of them claimed to hold the truth, but not a single person considered that they collectively held the truth.

- If you've seen the movie *A Few Good Men* (1992, Sony Pictures, dir. by Rob Reiner) you undoubtedly remember the famous scene when Col. Jessep (Jack Nicholson) is cross examined by military lawyer Lt. Kaffee (Tom Cruise) and in frustration explodes, "You can't handle the truth!" Is it possible that there's a side to the story that we prefer not to hear or give credence to because it hurts too much?

- Although we need to keep our minds open, remember the adage: If you open your mind too much your brains will fall out. As with most things in life, it comes down to a balance.

- When we need to make a decision, do we take all sides of the story, even our own, into account? Our own story is what we know as intuition, or gut instinct, which carries all the knowledge we have gleaned in our lifetime, consciously and unconsciously, and which we hold from our ancestors. Instinct is an important aspect of decision making and shouldn't be dismissed.

# 13 WHAT DO YOU KNOW ABOUT ANGER?

*Mine and Mind your GOALS to achieve*
*Greater Opportunities and Living Standards.*

IN 1993 THERE WAS a violent six-month strike in the U.S. involving the largest coal company in the world and its unionized workers. I was told that it was the first time in U.S. mining history that supervisors had crossed the picket lines to keep the mine operating. Naturally, the union members felt betrayed and, as tensions and hostilities rose, at least two supervisors' homes were burned to the ground.

Mining is an industry based on trust between the workers, with miners working deep underground in extremely close quarters and looking out for each other in dangerous working conditions. These miners and supervisors lived in the same towns, their children went to the same schools, and their families attended the same churches. Imagine the betrayal the ordinary workers on strike must have felt as they watched their neighbours and mining brethren in management cross the picket lines every day.

My colleague Tom Colosi, then vice president of

> **Mining is an industry based on trust between the workers.**

national affairs with the American Arbitration Association, was hired by the mining company to conduct a post-strike conflict resolution exercise, which was the first time this type of intervention had been used anywhere in North America.

When Tom called me from his office in Washington, D.C., he said he was seeking the 10 best people he knew in ADR who were up to the challenge of this assignment. I was the only Canadian invited to join the group. Tom said he needed to know right away whether I was willing to participate if this exercise went ahead. Within a few days union members would vote on a new collective agreement, and Tom planned to assemble the conflict-resolution team on the night of the vote. If the new collective agreement passed, we would start our work the next day; if it did not, we would go home and all expenses would be covered. I told him I'd get back to him quickly.

It was a couple weeks before Christmas, and my stepdaughter had recently arrived at our house with her husband and two boys. Her husband had lost his job, as had many in his industry in that part of Canada, and the family needed a place to stay until he found work. Although there was already animosity between Mary and her son-in-law, I had taken a liking to him over the years and had spent time helping him work through the pain of his childhood issues and addictions.

Under these circumstances I was concerned about being away from home for the 10 days this assignment was expected to last, although I didn't tell Tom about the situation. However, my wife encouraged me to go; she knew Tom and his wife Susan, and believed this was an opportunity to further my commitment and growing expertise in the ADR field.

I agreed to go and thanked Tom for the great privilege of working with him. However, I was in turmoil over the trip; first, because of the situation at home, and second, because I wondered if I was up to this enormous task. I didn't want to disappoint Tom or the other team members whom I had not yet met.

On the night the vote was to occur I flew into a city in Kentucky, harbouring a secret desire for the union to vote against the collective agreement! When the team met, Tom outlined the strategy, explaining that if by midnight the vote was successful we would start the next day. Each of us would then facilitate a dialogue with two groups, each including about 100 men. At midnight word came that the collective agreement had been accepted by the union membership, so this amazing undertaking was to commence the next morning.

I phoned home to let Mary know, and to find out what was going on at home. She told me she felt threatened by her son-in-law, which instantly aroused my anger. I was frustrated that I was so far away from home helping others when my family clearly needed me. She advised me to focus on what I was doing, and if anything happened she'd call me immediately. There was no way to know how long this assignment would actually last; we just had to take it one day at a time. I went to bed searching for inner peace, trusting that all was meant to be and that I was where I was supposed to be.

The next morning we headed to meet with management. Before the meeting started I noticed the president of the company, and I approached him to express my gratitude that top management was willing to hold such an innovative conflict resolution intervention for the well-being of the employees. I asked him what had prompted him to consider such a process, and he shared a personal story about how his daughter had run away from home when she was a teenager, and how he and his wife had prayed for her safe return. It took three years, but eventually she came home, went to university, became a professional and started her own family. I was deeply touched, both by the story and by the fact that he would share it with me. I couldn't help thinking about my own family in disarray at the time. He said he understood there was pain and anger among the miners, and he wanted to do something to help them heal. There's much more to mining than just running a business, he said; it was about caring for people.

The meeting was called to order and Tom explained how the program would be conducted. One by one, each team member stood and Tom introduced us to the group. When I stood up, Tom said, "That's Ernie. You will come to see his humanity." His words surprised me but also anchored

## A man pointed at me and shouted, "What do you know about anger?"

me in the moment, which was just what I needed.

When it was time to divide into groups, the eight team members were shuffled into large break out rooms and the men filed in. I stood at the front facing about 100 men, and behind me were a blackboard and flip chart. The room was dead silent and I could see the anger on their faces. I had an unsettling feeling that this was not going to work out well. I caught myself, realizing I needed to forget my own troubles and just do my job.

I extended greetings. No response.

I explained I was there to listen and allow them to vent about what had happened during the strike. I told them it was important to explore their feelings before everyone went back into the mines, and I asked if anyone would like to start.

Again, no response. In fact, it was totally quiet, like the calm before the storm. It seemed I stood there for a long time without hearing any sound. I wondered if I would be embarrassed if nothing came out of this session.

"I realize that many of you must be angry," I said, deciding to venture a bit further. "Would you like to express the feelings behind that anger?" I had learned from a great

Mohawk social worker that an important element of anger management is getting to the feelings that can cause anger. It can be a painful journey but it's necessary.

All of a sudden, a man sitting in the front row pounded the desk with his fist, pointed accusingly at me and shouted, "What do you know about anger?"

I was absolutely startled and thrown totally off guard. In an instant, all my frustration over the troubled situation at home boiled over and I forgot where I was. Before I knew it I was yelling back at him. "You want to know what I know about anger? Well, I'll tell you *exactly* what I know about anger!"

I ranted on, describing in great detail the problems at home and how our son-in-law was threatening and intimidating his mother. "So what the hell am I doing here when I should be

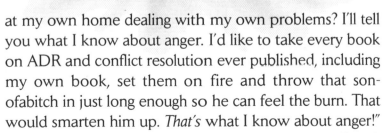

at my own home dealing with my own problems? I'll tell you what I know about anger. I'd like to take every book on ADR and conflict resolution ever published, including my own book, set them on fire and throw that son-ofabitch in just long enough so he can feel the burn. That would smarten him up. *That's* what I know about anger!"

I remember the relief I felt when I finished, yet I realized how totally out of touch I was with my surroundings. The next instant, the room erupted into applause, whooping and laughter, and the men pounded on the desks with approval. As I gradually regained my composure I saw that the men no longer looked angry but were clearly wondering what to do next. In mediation terms this is often called the "dark moment" of the mediation, when even the mediator is unsure what the next step will be. I searched for some way to bring light to the moment.

"Thank you, men, for listening to my anger," I said. "Thank you for letting me safely vent my feelings, my hurts and pains. I truly am grateful, and I can now focus on what I'm here for. For me the question is, what do I do with my anger now that it's been revealed? When you go home and go underground into the mine, what will you do with your anger?"

The room was quiet, but this time the atmosphere was solemn rather than sad. An idea came to me.

"Does anyone have a paper clip?" I asked. I'm sure they were wondering why on earth I would want a paper clip at a moment like this, but one was found among the group and passed to me. I held it up.

"See this paper clip?" I said. "What can you do with it?"

There were chuckles, and someone answered, "You can clip papers together."

"And what else?" I urged. "Think about it. Use your imagination. What else can you do with a paper clip?"

After a few moments, someone called out, "You could clip your tie to your shirt." That was all it took to start a flood of ideas. The men were shouting out so many suggestions that I struggled to record them all on the flip chart and blackboard. When the group quieted down I counted 40 things on our list.

"C'mon," I urged. "C'mon, let's get to 50."

The men were now very energized, and they played the best paper clip game I had ever seen, working together as a group to list 50 different things you can do with a paper clip. Some of the suggestions were very funny and there were plenty of jokes flying. The final idea, "You can pick your nose with it," drew roars of laughter.

When we were finished I stood back and read out the list. "A paper clip appears to have only one function," I said to the group, "but when you thought about it you identified at least 50 uses, and there may be more. So now the question is, what can you do with your anger—other than the usual things that come to mind, which are mostly violent? I want you to use your imagination again, and let's talk about other things we can do with anger."

For two hours we had a fantastic dialogue and I wrote pages and pages of flip chart notes. To end the session I told them about the evening I spent talking with my wife's son-in-law about his life challenges, trying to help him see things differently. I asked him several questions, including whether he could see under his nose.

## In the absolute blackness of the mine I realized how daring these men were.

Of course the answer to that question is no. I explained that we were created so that we can't see under our own noses, although we can see all around us and even inside ourselves. So we need others to tell us what's under our own noses—not as criticisms but as observations to help us see what's going on. He said it was the most profound conversation he'd ever had. I told the group that this conflict resolution intervention was sort of like that, since it would provide feedback to the mine owners about what was happening in the mines.

The team assembled that night to compare notes. The miners would be back at work the following day and we were scheduled to meet with them first thing in the morning. The team members were asked if we'd be willing to go down into the mines to talk to the workers, and three of us agreed to go. I felt that to hear the miners' side of the story I needed to go where they worked every day.

The three of us were picked up at 3 a.m. (my favourite time of day) so we'd be there for the start of the morning shift. We first rode the elevator down a few storeys, and then rode in a buggy for about 45 minutes to the face of the mine. I'll never forget when the supervisor stopped the buggy, turned off the lights for a moment, and explained that we were in the darkest place on earth. In the absolute blackness of the mine I realized how daring these men were and how they must have to trust each other—all the more reason for this incredible post-strike conflict resolution process.

When the miners took a break around 7 a.m. the supervisors introduced me, and I asked the men if they would share their thoughts and feelings with me. I had no paper or pen, yet I was confident that I could remember what I heard. I wanted to spend time with them and hear what they were thinking, just as I had done above ground with the supervisors and management. They very much respected that I had come to see them deep underground.

After a while the supervisor who had brought me to the mine said he was leaving, and added that I had to go too since I could not be left without supervision, but I said I had not spent enough time with the workers to know their concerns. A tall African-American miner intervened and said, "Don't worry about Ernie. Us union guys will take care of him."

I sat near the face of the mine and each miner took a turn to talk with me briefly. The miners brought me chewing tobacco and told me it helped ease mouth dryness in the mine. There were different types of chewing tobacco for different parts of the mouth, they said, and advised me to try every type just to be sure that my mouth didn't dry out. It was only when I became dizzy from all the tobacco that they finally admitted they had been joking with me; it wasn't true that there were different tobaccos for different parts of the mouth! Once again I had experienced humour in the most bizarre of places. I'd learned if you are teased you are liked, so I felt well loved. When I got back to the hotel room I wrote up all that I remembered the miners had told me and sent it to Tom, who added it to the team feedback.

On Thursday night the team assembled again and we were told that on Friday evening we'd be flown home for the weekend. I was anxious to return home, but since Ottawa was much too far away for a weekend trip I suggested to Tom that I leave on Friday and not return. He told me it was too early to end my involvement, and asked me to stay onsite through the weekend just in case there were issues. When I said I didn't want to be away from my wife that long, the company very generously arranged to fly her to Kentucky for the weekend.

The next day a new crisis arose over the question of when paid time began. Remember the elevator ride down, followed by the 45-minute drive to the front of the mine? The union took the position that paid time began before the elevator ride, once the miners were dressed and entering the elevator. The company took the position that paid time began after the buggy ride, once the miners had arrived at the front of the mine. With all the mine locations across the U.S., all the miners, and all the shifts, this was a major issue with big money at stake. I wondered how the collective agreement could not be clear on this point, but when I read the wording I saw it was open to interpretation. A wildcat strike was rumoured if this issue was not solved.

The mine manager and union rep at the mine asked my opinion, and I suggested that this was a matter for the company and union to figure out. Just for fun, however, I suggested a role play. The mine manager would pretend he was president of the union, the union rep would pretend he was president of the company, and I would be the mediator. They both joked that they couldn't possibly switch roles and think that way, but at my urging they did so. Lo and behold, during their role play they came up with an idea to solve the paid time issue. I passed their suggestion to Tom, and he in turn passed it along to the company and union. Everyone accepted the idea these two gentlemen had come up with. It was further affirmation of the value of these processes, and a tribute to those two men to be able to think it through that way.

The weekend was a very enjoyable respite and I was pleased that Mary was able to get away from the tension at home. The next week we met with all levels of the company and union, including the labour relations department, a full-time staff that dealt with grievances under the collective agreement all across the country. With their comprehensive filing and computer system they tracked every clause in the collective agreement, how each grievance was arbitrated, and which arbitrators made what kind of decision. One of them joked that if this conflict resolution stuff caught on they'd have far less work to do. This indeed is a universal truth about how non-adversarial options often challenge bureaucracies. I couldn't help but notice the difference between the swank offices of the labour relations department and the dark, dangerous environment in which the miners worked.

One very fascinating aspect of the new collective agreement was a conflict resolution committee, funded by the company, which would include both union and management. The committee would meet regularly to proactively deal with issues as they arose, thereby avoiding last-minute negotiations at the end of the collective agreement, avoiding strikes, reducing grievance arbitrations and moving towards grievance mediation.

That night we learned that both the company and the union were very satisfied with the results and we'd be going home the next day, earlier than expected. I discovered, however, that to change my flight I would have to make many more connections to get back to Ottawa, and I wondered aloud if I should wait until I could get a flight with fewer connections. One of the team members told me, "Ernie, just go. Go forward, from one airport to another until you get home. Don't wait for that one best flight."

What great advice that was; it was like a teach piece on problem solving. In football we're wowed by the quarterback who throws a Hail Mary pass rather than marching down the field, play by play. In baseball we cheer more loudly for home runs than for singles and doubles. Similarly, in problem solving we often look for the big solution, but just as much progress can be made by taking it one step at a time. It was a great principle with which to end this trip.

When I got home I had a good chat with the son-in-law, and told him how I'd reacted to the men in that room because of my frustration and anger. He said he respected me for being so honest about my feelings, while still caring for him at the same time.

## SOME LESSONS

● It's important to remember that personal matters are at stake in every dispute, even though they may not be obvious. Tom told me a story about an engineer who went to visit the contractor building a bridge. Throughout the conversation the engineer kept insisting that they learn about each other's lives, while the contractor simply wanted to discuss how they would build the bridge. In frustration, the contractor finally asked the engineer why he was dwelling on personal matters. The engineer said he knew the contractor had lots of technical expertise in building bridges, but without a bridge of communications between them they would have a much harder time solving any problems that arose. I've learned that if you get to know someone personally and learn their story, you're less likely to be angry at that person in a disagreement. Personalities affect outcomes as much as issues, so it's important to take the time to learn about the people around you.

● Even with large institutions, it's important to advance the potential of ADR in our society. In 1996 the OC Transpo public transit system in Ottawa endured a stressful 24-day strike. At the urging of my colleagues I wrote to the union and company leaders about this successful conflict resolution exercise that the coal company had conducted for miners after its strike. The response I received was that there was no need for that kind of approach. Three years later, in 1999, an OC Transpo employee went on a rampage at the head office, killing four people and then himself. During the public inquiry, Dave Brown of the *Ottawa Citizen* wrote a column on the value of conflict resolution processes, which I worked on with him behind the scenes.

When a conflict situation is settled, that's the best time to build in conflict prevention measures for the future, just to be sure that unresolved anger or festering bad feelings don't manifest themselves later. It seems that almost every week we hear another story of incomprehensible violence that has flared up in a workplace or family, when many of those tragedies could have been avoided with problem-solving techniques and processes. It's like a steam pipe with safety valves; if the safety valves don't have regular maintenance checks the pressure can build until the pipe explodes. Even if all seems quiet it's usually better to address issues upfront and ensure they don't linger. You don't want to realize too late that the quiet was simply the calm before the storm.

● This was the largest mining company in the world but the president of the company told me that for him it all came down to looking after individuals. In history, we tend to focus on the big issues, but often the most revealing stories are those of individual leaders on the world stage. Friedrich Hegel once said, "The only thing we learn from history is that we learn nothing from history," but I believe that only by knowing something about the individual leaders and their pathologies can we truly understand those historical events and their underlying causes. As Albert Einstein is reported to have said, "We can't solve problems by using the same kind of thinking we used when we created them." One major lesson from this story is one I learned at the outset of my ADR journey: remember to humanize both the knowledge and the issues.

# 14 CAN YOU APOLOGIZE AND MEAN IT?

*Incentive is what's in it for me; motivation is what's in me for it.*

CANADA'S TAINTED BLOOD scandal of the 1980s and 1990s was a public health disaster and one of the most complex issues in recent Canadian legal history. This tragedy has had many long-term consequences—medical, ethical, political and legal.

Many complicated factors contributed to this catastrophic situation, and among them was the delay in recognizing the risk of contracting HIV and hepatitis C through the blood supply. The AIDS epidemic had been on the public health radar since the early 1980s, yet Canada did not begin testing its blood supply for HIV until November 1985; it was reportedly among the last major industrialized nations to do so. In 1986, U.S. blood bank organizations began testing for hepatitis C, a debilitating liver disease, but Canada did not implement the test until 1990.

**Thousands died, and thousands more endured indescribable suffering.**

These decisions and non-decisions ultimately had a devastating cumulative effect. Between 1980 and 1985, at least 2,000 recipients of blood and blood products, most of them hemophiliacs, contracted HIV. Another 30,000 Canadians who had received transfusions between 1980 and 1990 were infected with hepatitis C. Thousands died, and thousands more endured indescribable suffering.

The legal mess dragged on for more than two decades. Monstrous class action litigation claims were filed in every jurisdiction in Canada. Huge sums were paid out in compensation by the federal government and many provincial governments. Many years later, following a five-year criminal investigation by the RCMP, criminal charges were filed against a former official with the Canadian Red Cross, two Health Canada doctors, and an official from a U.S. pharmaceutical company. In October 2007 all were acquitted of the criminal charges.

## The best place to be is the toughest place there is.

At the peak of the crisis in the 1990s, with the almost-daily revelations about this horrible tragedy, I was struck by the apparent absence of mediation efforts. With time of the essence, and given the huge number of parties and issues at stake, I knew that a formal ADR proposal would never see the light of day. But I believed, once again, that an ADR intervention could be of assistance, or at least would not cause further harm.

I was urged to get involved to whatever extent I could. I had already learned that the best place to be is the toughest place there is. So I initiated an informal, voluntary, citizen-based ADR undertaking with caring colleagues, *pro bono*, to make it clear from the outset that this was an impartial process. No one had asked us to do anything, and none of us was being paid.

Using the ADR Roundtable methodology, I approached two of the main parties to this horrendous situation: the senior counsel to the Canadian Red Cross, the organization administering the blood program at the time, and the chair of the Plaintiffs' Counsel of Canada on HIV Litigation, a national association that had been formed by plaintiffs' lawyers across Canada in response to the enormous number of lawsuits.

Both parties were invited to engage in a mediation process that would supplement, not supplant, the existing legal activities, and would not in any way interfere with the ongoing legal procedures. The invitation stressed that the process would be without prejudice, and would remain voluntary so that anyone could withdraw at any time, as long as they explained the reason to the mediator, to see if the reason for the withdrawal could be solved.

It took quite a bit of time to arrange a mediation session, since I understood that the insurance companies for the Canadian Red Cross were justifiably concerned about how the session would impact the legal proceedings and questions of liability. Eventually, however, a day-long session was scheduled to take place at my office with the senior counsel and an associate from the Canadian Red Cross and the chair of the plaintiffs' counsel group.

We had an extraordinary mediation session, during which many things transpired, emotionally, financially, and legally.

On an emotional level, parties on both sides were able to take off their official hats and connect as people. There were some very heartfelt personal moments as the individuals talked about the situation, not as representatives of institutions but as human beings. I saw that everyone in the room was visibly moved by the pain and grief that innocent people were facing as a result of this tragedy.

On the financial end, we were able to reach an agreement on one particular issue to lessen the financial burden on the complainants. By this time, many months into the scandal, the federal government had agreed to pay a fixed sum to those who had suffered as a result of the tainted blood products, but our mediation team had heard from complainants that the process was prohibitively complex. Applicants could stay within the class action lawsuits, but if they signed a full and final release they would immediately get some much-needed compensation. The catch, however, was that they were required to not only complete lengthy legal forms but also have the forms reviewed by a lawyer. Without this legal review they could not receive the fixed sum the government was willing to pay in exchange for a full and final release. What was most galling to the applicants was that lawyers were charging up to $2,000 for this review. To help expedite the settlement of these cases, during this mediation session it was agreed that up to $2,000 would be advanced to each applicant to help with legal costs.

> One question had always lingered: Who was at fault?

Finally, we also made progress legally. From the moment the situation had come to light one question had always lingered: Who was at fault? Was the Canadian Red Cross trying to cover its tracks and hiding behind the legal system? The suffering people wanted an apology from someone in authority, and I had seen from many previous situations how a sincere apology can help defuse a situation.

At our mediation session an apology was still a taboo subject since in those days apologizing was tantamount to an admission of liability. During our mediation session the lawyers from the Canadian Red Cross expressed, in human terms, how sorry they were at the suffering that had been caused. In an official capacity they also wanted to consider making an apology, but with no admission of liability. It was a breakthrough. I asked them if I could be the one to carry the message of "I'm sorry."

After that mediation session, I engaged in months of shuttle diplomacy to continue the negotiation efforts between the Canadian Red Cross and the plaintiffs' counsel group. During that time I also met with the executive director of the Ontario chapter of the Canadian Hemophilia Society, who had been given approval by the society's board to get involved in the ADR process. Over many months we met with men, women and children who were suffering and dying as a result of these tainted blood products. I cannot even begin to articulate their grief and their grievances. These encounters are indelibly imprinted on my mind and heart; they still energize me to carry on.

A preliminary facilitator's report was drafted and circulated, and then, after many months of shuttle diplomacy, a second report was issued outlining the outcomes of the ADR process. The report acknowledged that the Canadian Red Cross would consider an apology without admitting liability, but the placement of this acknowledgement in the report was negotiated.

The hemophilia society invited me to attend a meeting being convened in Toronto for the victims and their families. By consensus I was authorized by all parties to carry a message to the group, and I asked both the Canadian Red Cross and plaintiffs' association what that message should be. Did I have permission to say "I'm sorry"? Finally it was decided that my role would be to describe the ADR process that had taken place between the Canadian Red Cross, the plaintiffs' association and the hemophilia society, and tell the meeting attendees about the first two reports.

When it was my turn to speak, I said those things that I had been asked to say, and I also took the initiative to apologize on behalf of those at the Canadian Red Cross. I explained that the law had limits on what could be said officially, but on a human level they were very sorry about what had happened. I added, "The people at the Canadian Red Cross don't go to work every day saying 'who can I hurt today?'"

As I said those words, someone in the audience began heckling me but someone else called out, "Take it easy! This man had the courage to stand up and bring us an apology."

The class action lawyers eventually had me relegated to the side, but afterwards some people came to me privately and said they were glad to hear the apology. They said they had been afraid to speak up during the meeting because of the hostility in the room, but I appreciated that they took the time to share their gratitude.

Today many jurisdictions, including four Canadian provinces (B.C., Saskatchewan, Manitoba and Ontario), many U.S. states and Australia, have legislation that allows people to express sorrow for their actions without assuming legal liability.

I also want to share another story that highlights the immense difference that an apology can make:

### Car Accident—Death of a Child

A couple was driving in the car with their young daughter in the back seat. The father was driving, and the mother, eight months pregnant, sat in the front passenger seat. At an intersection a van sped through a red light and smashed into the front of the car. The couple and their daughter survived, but the baby was delivered stillborn.

To complicate this case even more, the driver of the van was an undercover police officer involved in a highspeed chase while driving a rented van, so there were lawyers from the Department of Justice for the police force, and a lawyer for the rental car company.

The couple went through many months of therapy, yet even so the father's anger was palpable. The litigation centred on damages, not liability. Apart from the huge financial hardship of missing work for an extended period, for the couple the biggest issue was that someone had killed their baby only a month before it was due to be born, and no one seemed to care. Worse, when they sought money to help with burial expenses for their stillborn child, the answer came back that in law, the unborn baby was considered a fetus and was not yet a human being!

This exacerbated the matter, as you can imagine, and I warned the insurance company that this attitude could increase the damages tenfold. Through the mediator it was suggested the insurance company pay an *ex gratia* payment, which is money paid without an admission of liability. Eventually a cheque arrived, without a cover letter and without a release, to help the couple pay the funeral and burial costs for their baby boy.

**What they really wanted was to hear him say he was sorry.**

The couple wanted to know if the driver of the van was sorry for what he did, but once again there were restrictions in the law on apologies. In addition, because of the complicated nature of the case and the physical distance separating the parties, there was no possibility that the parties could meet in a room for a mediation session.

So I suggested shuttle diplomacy, and over a period of months I spoke with the criminal defence counsel for the police officer who had been charged with careless driving. The couple had hoped he would be charged with a more major offence, but what they really wanted was to hear him say he was sorry.

At my suggestion the mother wrote a personal note to the police officer and included a picture of her baby boy who had died in her womb; the note was respectful and sought some explanation of how he felt about what he had done. The note and picture were passed on to the criminal defence counsel, who gave them to the officer.

The criminal defence lawyer later called me, and in a

tone that was unmistakably genuine, told me in detail how his client felt. The police officer, who had children of his own, had been tormented every day by this tragedy. He had been crying constantly since the accident and was receiving psychological help. He had wanted to personally apologize in the most profuse terms but had been told he could not admit to anything because of the litigation in the civil courts. His lawyer told me the officer wanted to thank the couple for the note and picture they had sent, and asked if I could pass on to them his profound apologies.

## Never let the law stand in the way of justice when we wish to honour our values.

I met with the couple and told them about the officer's apology. What I observed was phenomenal. The mother wept uncontrollably, lifted her head and hands upward and whispered, "Thank you." The father, who had become an alcoholic and was having trouble sleeping and working, broke down and cried. He shouted, "I thought every day of taking revenge on that police officer, a life for a life, and now 90 percent of my anger is gone. I feel like a new person again. I am so happy to know that he really was sorry for what he did. I can now let go of my anger."

The mother asked that I pass along to the officer how much his apology meant to them. In return they asked me to let the officer know that they forgave him and wished him well. For years, I kept the picture of that child by my desk as a reminder of what really counts at the most basic human level.

This sad case emphasized to me once again how important a sincere apology is in any dispute.

### SOME LESSONS

● There are so many challenges in making an apology— who says "I'm sorry" first? What if a person doesn't think they have done anything wrong, and there is nothing to apologize for? In another intervention I learned that in such cases one solution is to say "I'm sorry if anything I did or said offended you." If these words are said sincerely, it shows the other person that there is sensitivity to their pain, without having to worry about whether the cause of the pain was accidental, intentional, or even if the person making the apology believes any wrong has been committed.

I told this story to a colleague who was struggling with a situation in which his clients were stuck on the apology. He suggested this approach to them, and told me afterwards it had worked in allowing them to sincerely say "I'm sorry" without getting stuck on who was right or wrong.

- There are many ways to express a genuine apology, and we shouldn't give up trying even if there are seemingly impossible obstacles. The power of an apology can transcend many barriers.

- It took a long time for the law to change to allow people to apologize without being tarnished with legal liability. Even in my first year of practising law, and then again as I began my ADR journey, I concluded that we should never let the law stand in the way of justice when we wish to honour our values. Social movements have great power to change the laws. Sometimes the legislators are the last ones on board since they often don't act until they know the population is behind them. I remember someone gave me this quote: "Where did they go, how many are there, I must find them, I am their leader" (source unknown). It is important in a dispute for someone to lead the way and step into the fray in ways that touch hearts, not just pocketbooks.

- The news is full of stories of high-profile people who have publicly acknowledged their wrongdoing and apologized, and subsequently are given another chance. In the media this is called "getting in front of the story," but the same principle holds true in everyone's life. It's best to face the situation honestly, and as quickly as possible, so the failure to apologize does not make the conflict even worse—which it usually does.

- The story also raises other questions: Who is forgiveness for? Is it for the person receiving it or the one giving it? Does forgiveness come only after repentance, or is it a standalone ingredient of life when someone causes you pain? Much has been written about the power of forgiveness, and how learning to forgive can lift our own internal pain. This principle of forgiveness, including self-forgiveness, can often help in finding the answer to a problem. I like to say that the conflict will not be *re*solved, it will be *dis*solved.

- These stories characterize the power of restorative justice, a process that focuses on the accountability of the offender to the person who was harmed, rather than solely on the responsibility of the offender to the state. It humanizes the process by allowing the offender to acknowledge how the person was harmed. According to Ottawa police chief Vern White, who has conducted extensive research on this subject, "Restorative justice has resulted in a dramatic increase in victim satisfaction with the justice system. Among restorative justice cases a full 98 percent of victims say they are satisfied, compared with a 28 percent satisfaction rate in mainstream cases. This indicates the importance of victim-centred justice principles."

# 15 WHAT IS YOUR LANGUAGE REALLY SAYING?

*Don't kill two birds with one stone; rather, feed two birds in one nest.*

A MAJOR DEPARTMENT in the federal government was in a dispute with the national association of its employees. The conflict threatened to destabilize the whole agency and spark demonstrations and more disputes across the nation.

Both sides were humble and insightful enough to seek the assistance of a mediator to help them reach a solution and, after a lengthy cross-country search to find a mediator that was acceptable to both sides, I was recommended, interviewed and ultimately retained to conduct the mediation.

The phrase "take off the gloves" left a rather adversarial atmosphere.

The mediation was expected to last several months, given the complexity of the issues involved and the seemingly insurmountable obstacles, but everyone realized the potentially devastating effects of not reaching a solution.

Selecting the members of the mediation team is a critical aspect of the process. For parts of this intervention, I decided to bring in an experienced female colleague to help. I'd learned that the mediation team can sometimes be more effective with both genders, and in this case I determined that would be the case. Others were enlisted to provide technical expertise. Fortunately, all the negotiating team members on both sides were well-qualified problem solvers; some had been educated in Harvard programs, some were senior public servants, and others had a superior knowledge of traditional teachings, which was important since Aboriginal people and issues were a central part of this issue. I, too, had had extensive exposure to Aboriginal issues after being involved in various First Nations situations; in fact, this experience was among the reasons I had been recommended for this assignment.

At the beginning session with each side, I outlined the universal principles that I believed applied to this particular set of circumstances. One key point that I stressed was the use of language. I encouraged all parties to be aware of their own language and, as an example, told them the phrase that had come to me years earlier: "Don't kill two birds with one stone; rather, feed two birds in one nest."

Eventually, after caucusing separately a few times with each negotiating team, both sides agreed to meet for the first time and, as part of planning for the meeting it was important to properly set up the negotiating room. This is a detail that is sometimes forgotten or dismissed, but both sides must agree on seating arrangements and the placement of the table and chairs. During a discussion about these arrangements, a government official suggested a circular table, since circles are often associated with Aboriginal processes. However, the woman elder from the employee team wanted a rectangular table since she did not believe the parties were ready for a circular table in the first meeting. To help resolve this impasse, I asked if I could be allowed to identify when I thought the parties were "circle table ready," which they both agreed to. Adopting that phrase helped move the mediation process forward and again demonstrated the importance of language to this situation.

At that first meeting, four tables were set in a rectangular formation. As both parties had agreed, three members of the employee team sat on my left, three members of the government team sat on my right, and one member from each team sat across from me and my colleague.

The opening dialogue was fruitful, and by the end of that first morning a member of the employee team was already expressing how encouraged he felt about the progress.

"This is great," he announced, slapping the table. "I think on both sides we're getting close to the issues. It's now time to take off the gloves."

I sensed he was well intentioned in saying this, but I noticed the phrase "take off the gloves," with its implications of fisticuffs and confrontation, unexpectedly left a kind of adversarial atmosphere. The negotiations were at a critical juncture in a dispute that had simmered for years and had recently intensified, and I wondered if this comment would have any effect.

There was a thoughtful moment as participants paused to consider this suggestion. I decided to stay silent and defer to the atmosphere of reflection that I sensed had taken hold.

Finally someone on the employer side spoke up. "Remember what Ernie told us about the use of language?" he said. "Instead of 'taking off the gloves' why don't we 'roll up our sleeves'?"

Immediately the entire mood of the room changed and people smiled.

"I agree," said the person who had referred to gloves. "Let's roll up our sleeves."

I commended them for formulating an approach, listing the issues to be addressed, and agreeing on common language they could work with, all of which were good signs for the future. In fact, everyone then had lunch together, which was a first. There was still much to do, but there was a sense that progress had been made.

## Immediately the entire mood of the room changed and people smiled.

During those two days of the mediation session, I placed a blue plastic cup in front of me that was half filled with water. I had purposely chosen the colour blue to represent the idea of "blue sky thinking," which is often required in mediations. No one seemed to notice the cup and I never touched it, but its presence gave me inner peace and also reminded me of the importance of viewing every situation as half full rather than half empty. This was a particularly apt reminder in this mediation session given the importance of language.

Not long after that first two-day meeting, so much progress had been made that a follow-up meeting was needed to help wrap the issues into a comprehensive set of solutions. The government team members said they were ready for a second meeting, which felt good, so I went to the employee association side and delivered that message.

"We will have only one meeting," the woman elder said.

I was shocked. After all this progress, they weren't willing to meet a second time?

"I don't understand," I said. "How can you ever complete this discussion without another meeting?"

"Only one meeting," she repeated firmly.

I felt quite deflated. After all this momentum I could

not believe that there would be only one meeting. Had I missed something or done something wrong in managing this mediation? It was a confusing and defeating moment, but then I reminded myself that the feelings of the disputants were important and my feelings were not. So I corrected my attitude and took time to reflect.

I remembered what other Aboriginal elders had taught me: that understanding language means understanding not just the words but also the meaning of the words. I could recall many impasses in many disputes that had been caused by language. Sometimes, even though people speak the same language, they ascribe different meanings to words. There are further exasperations when people *don't* speak the same language and their words must be translated. Indeed, history is full of stories about conflicts caused by misunderstandings.

After all this reflection, I went back to the woman elder. "Please let me know what you meant by only one meeting," I said. "How can this dialogue continue without another gathering? I want to be sure I totally understand what you mean before I carry that message to the other side."

> Sometimes, even though people speak the same language they ascribe different meanings to words.

"We will get together again," she responded. "The idea of having one meeting and then another meeting causes a sense of separation of the dialogue, and we cannot have separate dialogues. So we will have one meeting under many moons."

To this day her words are indelibly fixed in my mind and heart, and I often quote them as one of the wisest phrases I have ever heard. I once again felt so lucky to be involved in ADR, and to constantly acquire such incredible insights from others.

I thanked her and went to the government with the message about having "one meeting under many moons," which was well received and resonated particularly well with the Aboriginal members of that team.

Everything was eventually resolved. There was no demonstration, no work stoppage, no litigation, no confrontation, and therefore also no media.

I am grateful to those negotiation teams for reaffirming for me the value of these mediation principles. They all were positive in their comments about that mediation experience, which does not always happen. I am glad to be able to write about it now.

## SOME LESSONS

- Words can be loving or lethal, and like a bullet fired from a weapon, once the words are said they cannot be recalled. Cupid's arrows are associated with falling in love but an arrow can also be used to harm. We must each choose carefully what words we use since thoughtless words flung carelessly can cause permanent damage. In our fast-paced world of instant communication, the touch of a button can launch not only a war of words but also a war of weapons. I like the expression "Put your brain in gear before you put your mouth in motion."

- We all need opportunities to be creative, so why not in our language? There is more than one way to make a point or deliver a message. Just as our computers give us warning messages before we perform certain transactions, I try to have a warning message pop up in my head before I speak: Are you sure you want to perform this transaction? It's been suggested that when we need to vent we should write down the words and throw away the paper. Perhaps we should try the same tactic with our thoughts or feelings before they metamorphose into words.

● There's no doubt that words hurled in anger can hurt or incite a reaction, so I've tried to find ways to remain steady and calm when they're hurled at me. The grand chief taught me about the "seven skins" you develop over time with conflict. I heard about a technique that one group uses to defuse a conflict: the individuals in the dispute stand facing each other at a safe distance, each taking turns to yell, scream, and swear at the other person. Standing nearby are community observers who assure the disputants that the words have been fully heard. The session ends when the disputants get tired and run out of steam—or burst into laughter.

# 16 HOW DO YOU PERSEVERE THROUGH LIFE'S HARDSHIPS?

*Rather than complain about what you don't have and use it as an excuse, be grateful for what you do have and regard it as a blessing.*

MY INVOLVEMENT with issues affecting persons with disabilities began in the late 1960s. While I was attending university I taught English part time to 10 disabled students in grades 9, 10, and 11. In fact, there was only one student in grade 11, Rod Carpenter, who was born with cerebral palsy but had a fine mind and a sense of humour, and with the help of his family he was able to deal with his unique struggles in life. He managed his electric wheelchair with his fingers and communicated primarily by typing on a computer keyboard with a rod mounted on a headband.

**There are many forms of disability, both visible and invisible.**

That teaching assignment permanently affected how I view life, and I found myself trying to understand how someone could cope with such enormous obstacles. One day I asked Rod how it felt not to be able to walk. He replied by asking me how I felt not being able to fly. I said I didn't know because I've never flown. He said it was the same for him; he'd never walked. His disability was obvious, he said, but there are many forms of disability, both visible and invisible. This conversation helped me see the world in a different light.

In 1979 Rod asked me what we were going to do for the United Nations International Year of Disabled Persons in 1981. Until then I hadn't known that event was coming up, but as it turned out we celebrated International Year of Disabled Persons by creating Reach Canada (www.reach.ca) a charitable organization that provides *pro bono* legal services and educational programs for issues around disabilities. Our first Reach project, which garnered national headlines, was to create a precedent so that disabled persons who could not write could use facsimile signatures and registered thumbprints for bank accounts and credit cards in their own names. It took about two years to negotiate with the Bank of Montreal to find co-operative and creative ways around the legal and regulatory obstacles, but eventually the bank implemented this new policy, and all the other major banks followed suit over the years. It was a remarkable experience in achieving social justice for all segments of society, especially those who are the most vulnerable, and reminds us that we have all gained from the field of disability through access to new technologies and better access to justice.

I mention this story to provide some background to my involvement in issues concerning people with disabilities, and to give some context to the central story of this chapter:

One day at a charitable event I was approached by a woman named Pat and her daughter, Ana, who had cerebral palsy and was in a wheel chair. Pat said she remembered me from Reach and said she urgently needed to talk with me. A few days later she came to my office and told me she had terminal cancer and had been given only a short time to live. She and her husband, Paul, were separated, and Paul was living in the finished basement of their house. Pat said she was moving to her own place since her health did not permit her to care for Ana. Paul was now going to be the main caregiver—and soon the only caregiver.

Pat wanted to ensure that she and Paul had a separation agreement in place before she died so that all the complex legal and financial matters could be settled. She wanted my help, but knew Paul would be suspicious of any mediation because they'd had a bad experience with a supposedly neutral therapist who'd ended up siding with Pat. Although Pat didn't disagree with that criticism, she was afraid if they didn't find a mediator Paul could work with, she would die without settling their affairs. Pat sobbed as she handed me a handwritten note from Ana. The note, addressed to "Mr. Mediator," pleaded with me to help her parents sort out their dispute since they were all under enormous stress watching her mother die.

I met with Paul, he agreed to participate, and after many months and many sessions Pat and Paul eventually signed a separation agreement. I remember they shook hands at the last session, pleasantly surprised that they had managed to agree. I commended them for what they

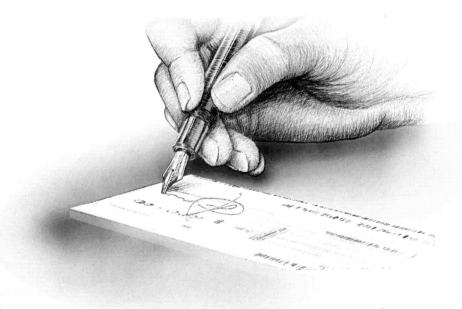

had accomplished in such dire circumstances and with a forced timetable.

Afterward Paul admitted privately that he was astonished that he had come to trust me and the mediation process, and asked me what made me "tick" as a mediator. I was reluctant to tell him about the very spiritual core belief system that guided me since I knew Paul was an avowed atheist. I tried to avoid answering, but Paul was so insistent that I finally told him how I'd read long ago that the Bible said that Jesus was a mediator, and that I'd left my flourishing law practice to find out what this mediation stuff was all about. He said he was astounded that someone with my knowledge and skills could believe such ridiculous notions, and said he'd work on changing my beliefs.

After Pat passed away, a conflict arose several months later between Paul and the trustees of Pat's estate over the management of the estate and the limited trust funds. Litigation ensued, and I served as the solicitor for Paul and Ana, with Paul as Ana's litigation guardian since she was not yet of legal age. I saw firsthand how the situation upset Ana. Eventually, after court-annexed mediation, the trustees agreed to resign in favour of new trustees but the case was very unsettling for everyone. I admired Ana and her father for their determination to carry on, but I couldn't help but wonder how they could persevere despite almost unbearable complications.

## I couldn't help but wonder how they could persevere despite almost unbearable complications.

Paul then became involved in a relationship with Agnes, who was also diagnosed with cancer. Although she persevered with a positive attitude Ana soon lost a stepmother and Paul a loving partner. Unfortunately there had been some animosity between Paul and Agnes' family so the family did not tell Paul when Agnes passed away, and later there were some estate issues involving Paul. For Ana, there was yet another death and another conflict, but through negotiation everything was settled.

Ana endured many obstacles over the next few years, and as she persevered I helped her negotiate, mediate, and litigate many issues just so that she could cope in this world and have equality. At one point she decided to be baptized a Christian. Although Paul vehemently disagreed with religious things he honoured her decision. It was yet another issue for the two of them to sort out, however, which they did through discussion, sometimes with me as intermediary at the beginning.

> For Ana, there was yet another death and another conflict.

At age 21 Ana was forced to leave the Ontario high school system but she needed to go to adult high school to complete her credits. The only adult high school in Ottawa, however, was a large, older building that was not accessible for persons with disabilities; the washroom was not accessible and there was no budget for an assistant, which Ana needed to get around, take notes and assist with the washroom. This new obstacle had put her entire life path in jeopardy.

Ironically, Ontario premier Dalton McGuinty had earlier made a majestic speech in the Ontario legislature extolling the new *Accessibility for Ontarians with Disabilities Act*, which required equal access and accommodation for persons with disabilities. Yet Ana was facing a hurdle that was profoundly affecting her ability to finish her education equal with other Ontario residents.

I got involved as her solicitor to help resolve this situation. There were several rounds of negotiations that lasted for months, involving the school board trustee, the principal of the adult high school, and the premier's executive assistant. Every conceivable possibility was considered to get beyond the legal and physical impediments, but no solution was in sight.

Finally I asked that the parties meet in a face-to-face meeting, which I felt was important as I'd come to see that breakthroughs often result when people are together in the same room and have the attitude that a solution can be found. At the meeting were the school board super-intendent and the lawyer for the school board, whom I knew to be fair-minded from my dealings with him on another matter. Ana allowed me to tell her story about her life challenges; the school board representatives were clearly touched and I knew they wanted to find a solution. Occupational therapists had already identified all the high school's deficiencies for access by disabled persons, and when I mentioned that these obstacles stood in the way of Ana's rights under the new legislation, the board lawyer said, "Thanks, Ernie, I now can think of a way to resolve this on the basis of the legal duty to accommodate." This was a public facility that had to comply with the new leg-islation, so the washroom was built and funding was allo-cated for an assistant. But of course one solution leads to another problem.

A concern was expressed over whether the assistant would always be available to help Ana in the washroom, so the suggestion was made that she use the washroom at specified times. Paul and Ana called this idea absurd, and the others knew it was not natural. But instead of ridiculing the idea I went back to the basics of equality, and said that since everyone was now equal under the law, if Ana had to go to the bathroom at specified times of day, every other person at the school would have to as well. That idea was quickly set aside, and a way was found

> **Instead of ridiculing the idea, I went back to the basics of equality.**

to allow Ana the dignity to attend to her needs with technology and logistics, which would help people in similar circumstances in the future.

Ana successfully completed adult high school, with commendations, and enrolled at a college. In her second year she was accepted into the full-time residence for students with disabilities.

I recall listening to a CBC radio interview that had been conducted with Ana when she was about 10 years old. She and other children with disabilities were asked how they cope. At one point they each talked about how they had considered themselves a burden to their families and openly discussed that they had considered committing suicide at different times. Eventually, though, each of these youngsters accepted their plight in life and found the strength to persevere. It is a very compelling interview.

I remain very close to Ana and her father Paul. Before Pat passed away she gave me permission to tell the story of the daughter who was the focus of her whole life.

## SOME LESSONS

● It's important to have a healthy attitude to deal with the problems in life. We all face setbacks and failures, and learning to accept, deal with, and overcome our individual challenges is part of developing what we like to call "character." I've seen in mediations that when the parties approach everything with a negative attitude there's less chance to solve the problem since negativity can block ideas from flowing.

● Someone once told me about a media baron's explanation of how the media made profits: before people go to bed at night, they want to hear that others had a worse day than they did, and when they get up in the morning, they want to hear that someone else had a worse night. In the media business, "if it bleeds, it leads."

But of course good things happen every day and most are unreported. I had an experience with a group of young people who settled their differences without worsening the conflict, which could easily have occurred, but I could not get the media to pay attention to these youths and give them credit for their non-violent problem solving. In my frustration, it occurred to me that with today's instantaneous news it's hard to report on an intelligent and long-lasting initiative, especially if there are no images. In Australia the Conflict Resolution Network gives out awards to media outlets reporting stories that help people understand how to generate solutions, not further the conflict.

● This story highlights an important element that we often see in negotiations, called Best Alternative to a Negotiated Agreement (BATNA). This refers to a solution that seems unacceptable yet is better than the alternatives. One person in a mediation described it perfectly when he said, "I don't like this deal but I can live with it, and the other options are worse." In this story about Ana, the official found it unacceptable that Ana would be able to go to the washroom at any time, and proposed that instead she go at specified times. When I reminded him that equality under the law meant that everyone in the school would then have to go to the washroom at a specified time, the person realized that solution was worse than the one he had considered unacceptable, and ultimately he accepted the "unacceptable" option.

● There's a story, which you may have heard, about a man who decided to swim across Lake Ontario. When he was halfway across, he felt too tired to complete the swim so he turned around and headed back. We sometimes take this same attitude to problem solving. We say we have no energy to deal with the problem, or we procrastinate in dealing with it (Why put off until tomorrow what you can put off until the day after tomorrow?). However, it sometimes takes more energy to work around the problem than it would to solve it.

● It's human nature to want to blame others for your misfortune. Through some friends I learned about the Course of Miracles, a spiritual set of teachings on dealing with life's challenges. One lesson teaches that when you are upset, rather than blame someone else you should view that as an opportunity to understand something about yourself.

Many years ago I had a fascinating client, an elderly woman in her 80s who said she wanted to sue her two former husbands. I asked her what she would sue them for, as I could not see what the cause of action would be. Eventually it emerged that she had persevered through a lot, yet had ended up alone and destitute. When I suggested her complaint was really against God she responded, "OK, so how do I go after God?" It was a very enlightening moment; how could I not feel anything but affection for her? I referred her to therapy for the elderly, as I'd heard that unresolved hurt, guilt or anger can fester and become a bigger problem later in life.

# 17 ARE YOU SURE EVERY ISSUE IS ON THE LIST?

*From an acorn does an oak tree grow.*

ONE SUNDAY AFTERNOON my step-daughter asked me to stay with her two young boys, then about six and eight years of age, for a couple of hours while she went out with her mother. Naturally I told her I would be honoured to do so, and to entertain the boys I decided to make up a game called ADR. (Really!)

"What's ADR, Giddo?" the older one asked, addressing me by the Arabic name for grandfather.

"ADR is alternative dispute resolution, and it helps us solve problems and disputes," I explained. "There are always many different ways to do that, and the idea is to find the way that is best for everyone."

> "Remember, there's one very important rule: we all have to agree."

I told them that our mis sion in this ADR game was to decide how we would spend a whole day together, even though we had only two hours. I introduced them to brainstorming and explained that during brainstorming, everyone can contribute ideas without anybody else interrupting or saying anything bad about their idea.

So together we made a very long list of all the things we could do together that day; in fact by the time our list was complete the three of us had listed about 60 different ideas.

I told them that next we each had to decide which activities were the most important to us and mark those as "A" activities. Each of us independently assigned A, B, or C to every idea on the entire list without any discussion.

When we compared results, there were about 10 "A" activities. We had already come quite far in this game but our two hours were nearly up, and we were soon expecting the boys' mother and grandmother to come home.

But the boys' mom called soon afterward to ask if I would mind spending the rest of the day with the boys since she was really enjoying spending time with her mother. Of course I agreed.

When I got off the phone I told the boys we were going to be together the rest of the afternoon. "So now we can keep playing the ADR game!" I added.

"What do you mean, Giddo?" they asked.

"Well, now we have a list of 10 things we can do together this afternoon. But since it's wintertime in Ottawa we can probably do only three of those things. So now we have to all talk about all of those activities and decide which three we're going to do. This is called "consensus," and that means we will have to negotiate until we finally agree on what activities we'll do today. Remember that there's one very important rule: we all have to agree. Do you think we can do that?"

Both boys nodded, so the three of us took time to discuss all 10 options, using the fighting fair principles (included at the end of this chapter) from the Australian Conflict Resolution Network. The final three choices were to see a movie, go out to eat, and come back to build a snowman.

So off we went at about noon with the goal of completing our three activities by 5:00, when their mother and grandmother intended to return.

We enjoyed a wonderful afternoon seeing a movie, eating out, and finally returning to the house and building a snowman. They had lots of energy—and I was reminded once again how much energy is required to raise children!

## I was exhausted from all the activity, and we still had a half hour left.

By 4:30 we had completed the three activities that we had all agreed on, and had also shared a productive day with lessons on communication, negotiation, compromise, and decision making by consensus. The two boys were still going strong, but I was exhausted from all the activity and we still had a half-hour left before their mother and grandmother were expected to return.

"OK, boys, Giddo is going to lie down and rest for half an hour before your mom and nanny get home," I said, already imagining a few moments of rest.

"Giddo, you can't do that!" insisted the older boy.

"But why not?" I asked, surprised at his response.

"Because it's not on the list!"

I laughed out loud and hugged the boys, realizing that I had learned yet another valuable lesson from the children, which I call "the list is never closed." In mediation, and in life, it's important to allow everyone to add something to the list and let their voice be heard. I thanked the boys for this insight—and took my half-hour rest!

I often share this story in training, mediation and other ADR interventions since it's a perfect example of how we can learn valuable lessons from unexpected experiences.

## SOME LESSONS

● It's never too early to teach children about subjects we might think are too adult. By creating an ADR game I was able to share valuable principles of life with the children in ways that were both fun and educational.

● Sometimes in our discussions we set conditions, give ultimatums, or refuse to talk about an issue (someone once said to me in a mediation, "I will not give life to that issue!") Instead of closing the discussion in this way, it's important to agree that anyone can add a new item to the list at any time—otherwise there will be no complete list. If anyone is permitted to veto another's concerns, then conflict continues, festers and worsens. Try keeping the list open for new additions and see what happens. Whenever I write an agenda I add "Other issues" as the last item so that those attending the meeting know there will always be time to discuss issues they feel are important.

● One day the mother of these two young boys asked me to speak to them about how they were not helping her with all the things she did for them around the house. I wasn't sure what I was going to say, but when I met with them I asked them to play a game. First, I asked them to breathe out without stopping for as long as they could, and they blew and blew until their faces were red and they couldn't blow anymore. Then I asked them to breathe in without stopping, and they gave it a valiant effort, breathing in until they couldn't stand it anymore. "What would happen if you didn't breathe in and breathe out?" I asked. One of the boys promptly answered, "We'd die." That gave me a great lead into a lesson. "Well, then," I said, "you know that when you breathe in you take in oxygen from nature, which is how we survive, and when you breathe out you give carbon dioxide back to nature, which is how nature survives. With nature we need to have both give and take, and without both of those processes you would die. The same thing happens with relationships between people. If there isn't both give and take, the relationship will also die." They thought about this for a moment, and it seemed to strike a chord. "Why are you telling us this?" the older boy asked, which was the opening for a discussion on what they took from their mother. I asked them to tell me all the things their mother did for them. I wrote them all down, and of course it ended up being a very long list. Then I asked them to list what they did for their mother, and they had trouble thinking of anything! Finally I asked them to tell me what chores their mother had asked them to do around the house, and that list was also quite long. We then compared the three lists, and I asked them, "Do you think that in your house, there is give and take between what your mother does for you and what you do for her?" There was a solemn "no" from both boys and they agreed they would try harder to give more to their mom and not just take.

I have always thought of this as a very pertinent lesson because if we didn't have this give-and-take relationship with nature we would not survive. I often share this principle in discussions about how people deal with one another and solve problems—as individuals, in institutions, and even as an extended human family.

- Whatever activities are on the list, it's important to build in some time for rest right from the beginning so that everyone will have the energy to finish the list. Rest is important in mediation situations, too. For example, after the parties have reached an agreement I always encourage both parties to "sleep on it" before signing.

If the parties have time for rest and reflection, and are not rushed into signing, they are much more likely to honour and comply with the agreement.

## FIGHTING FAIR PRINCIPLES

**Do I want to resolve the conflict?**
Be willing to fix the problem.

**Can I see the whole picture not just my own point of view?**
Broaden your outlook.

**What are the needs and anxieties of everyone involved?**
Write them down.

**How can we make this fair?**
Negotiate.

**What are the possiblities?**
Think up as many solutions as you can. Pick the one that gives everyone more of what they want.

**Can we work it out together?**
Treat each other as equals.

**What am I feeling?**
Am I too emotional?
Could I...get more facts,
Take time out to calm down,
Tell them how I feel?

**What do I want to change?**
Be clear. Attack the problem, not the person.

**What opportunity can this bring?**
Work on the positives, not the negatives

**What is it like to be in their shoes?**
Do they know I understand them?

**Do we need a neutral third person?**
Could this help us to understand each other and create our own solutions?

**How can we both win?**
Work towards solutions where everyone's needs are respected.

© Conflict Resolution Network,
      PO Box 1016, Chatswood NSW 2057 Australia.
      www.crnhq.org

# 18 HOW IS YOUR STORY CONNECTED TO OTHER STORIES?

*Anyone's problem is everyone's problem.*

I'M ALWAYS FASCINATED when I hear someone say, "That's not my problem," and I try to understand this type of thinking. I've learned over the years that all problems in our world are interconnected in ways that we may not see until later, or indeed, may never fully comprehend.

Experts in many areas of study are continuing to prove that everything in this world is more connected that we realize. Physicists, for example, have formulated the chaos theory, which we popularly know as the butterfly effect, which shows how even the most insignificant event (the flap of a butterfly's wings) can have a large-scale effect on the entire system (whether or not there's a tornado in Texas). In the social sciences we have the famous phrase, "six degrees of separation," which grew out of the "small world" experiments back in the 1960s that attempted to measure the interconnectedness of human networks. We cannot deny that we are all

**We cannot deny that we are all connected through various kinds of networks.**

connected through various kinds of networks, both natural and technological. I have observed, however, that when people see their problems as independent from the problems of others, more chaos erupts.

The final chapter of this book is one story in my personal journey, which reached a dramatic threshold many years ago. This story illustrates the universal truth that anyone's problem is everyone's problem.

I began my law career focusing on criminal and civil litigation, and after several years and numerous trials I had developed quite a bit of confidence and some reputation. I enjoyed the thrust and parry of the courtroom, the excitement and adrenaline of the adversarial process, and the win-lose contests. I'd been trained well in this adversarial process through law school, articling and the bar exams, which in those days all focused on the adversarial makeup of our court system. My early training was then augmented by ongoing continuing legal education programs on the art of arguing court motions, cross examinations and trial advocacy, which allowed me to increasingly fine-tune the "attack" on a witness, which you often see in TV shows and movies. In an artful, thorough cross examination each question is like an Exocet missile aimed squarely at the witness, and designed to cause irreparable damage.

In one case I was the legal counsel for the wife and mother in a divorce proceeding involving a dispute over custody and access. The couple had one child, a young daughter whom they both loved, and each parent was seeking sole custody. The case was very emotional and was heading towards trial. These trials are the most difficult type, since judges prefer not to have to make a ruling on which parent will have custody of the child and which one will have access. I have always considered the terminology of "custody" and "access" to be inequitable, as it wrongly gives the child the impression that there are two tiers of parenthood. This debate continues today in many forms.

As part of the pre-trial process there is an examination for discovery, during which the lawyer for the plaintiff has an opportunity to ask questions of the defendant under oath, and vice versa. The lawyers for both sides then obtain the transcript of this procedure and use it to further strategize the case, seek a settlement, or prepare for the trial. During the examination for discovery in this particular case, I was aggressively questioning the father when he suddenly became very emotional and eventually broke down. "OK, I quit!" he said. "You win! You can have custody! I can't take this anymore!" He got up and left the room.

It was quite a stunning moment. My client thought I was a hero; I felt more like a bum, but of course I could not divulge my own feelings. I was very confused and tormented over what had just happened.

My client wanted to celebrate but I knew I had to recalibrate so I begged off with the explanation that I needed to complete the paperwork. Back at the office, I began to feel the weight of what I'd done to that husband and father. I truly felt as though I'd sunk to a new low as a person, although it seemed that I had risen higher in the profession. *What kind of person am I becoming?* I thought.

After several hours of increasing misery I contacted a very close friend and asked if we could meet. I told her I needed to talk with someone I could confide in—someone who could give me honest, non-judgemental feedback.

Without naming names, I described the case to her and told her what had occurred, and in very unflattering terms described how I felt. I told her that I respected the need for a structured system of confrontation with a decision maker to help those who cannot resolve their differences, and I saw there was also a need to create court precedents to assist in negotiating solutions in other situations. However, I found it disrespectful that lawyers were allowed to treat their fellow human beings so viciously. I remember in the book *How You Can Find Happiness During the Collapse of Western Civilization* the author, Robert J. Ringer, lamented that lawyers can plead anything they want, ask the most outrageous and hurtful questions, and get away with it all. What had the system done to me as a person? Who was I to reduce another person to tears and focus solely on

## Despite my apparent outward success, that day I felt like a failure inside.

defeating the other side, especially when there was a child involved? I truly felt horrible.

My friend told me she was glad I was finally coming to grips with what I was feeling as she'd noticed over the past year how dissatisfied I'd become with this area of the law. I knew it was time for me to rethink what I should be doing as a lawyer. Despite my apparent outward success, that day I felt like a failure inside. I thanked her for our talk, and when I went home I spent the rest of the night alone, at times in tears, trying to figure out if there was any way I could apologize to that man and ask for his forgiveness. But of course I already knew that would be impossible; our system would not allow it.

I recalled a gathering of my colleagues at which one fellow complained how lousy he felt despite winning a major court case that day. When we asked him why, he replied, "Because my client won, someone else lost and I lost something of myself." At the time I had been bewildered by his response, but after my experience I could finally appreciate his outlook.

This incident and many other factors led me to explore ADR, and mediation in particular, especially in family law. In 1985 I ended my practice in litigation as a barrister but remained a solicitor. I never shy away from being a strong advocate in negotiating as a solicitor for a client, but no longer do any adversarial court-related work, unless it's a settlement conference, a case conference, or court-annexed mediation.

Many years into my ADR journey several of us were establishing the Canadian Institute of Conflict Resolution (CICR). A key advisor said he knew someone who would be a great asset to us, a well-connected gentleman who specialized in setting up complex events and organizations nationally and internationally. This person had expressed an interest in these ADR developments and had already said he wanted to meet me.

When the three of us met for lunch, I vaguely thought I recognized this gentleman but he didn't say anything so I let it go. My colleague and I were both impressed with him and were pleased when he agreed to act as a volunteer consultant. He spent many weeks interviewing people and doing research, and came up with a comprehensive proposal for the new CICR that he asked to present at a full session of all key stakeholders at Saint Paul University in Ottawa, where the CICR had its offices.

The classroom was packed when I arrived that day for the session, and everyone was eagerly anticipating this presentation. Everyone in the room was very accomplished in their respective professions, and we'd all been so impressed by the expertise of this consultant that we couldn't wait to hear what he had to say.

When the consultant rose to speak, he said he first wanted to explain why he had dedicated so much time to this project, despite his hectic schedule. Like everyone else, I was keen to hear about his motivation.

"Many years ago," he began, "I was involved in my own personal litigation and had an experience that is very relevant to why I am here today."

At that moment I was hit with the dreadful realization that I did know this person after all—he was the husband and father I had treated so badly in the cross examination many years ago. *He's here to get revenge,* I thought. I realized how clever this setup had been and how easily I had been duped. And now he would expose me—an apparent peacemaker, conflict resolution consultant, and mediator—as a litigation monster. In front of this group of my colleagues and supporters I'd be revealed as the embodiment of everything that the CICR was against—a wolf in sheep's clothing. I had always told my children that everything in life catches up with you, both the good and the bad, and now one of the worst experiences of my professional life had finally caught up with me. My heart pounded as I braced myself for the worst.

The consultant continued his story. "In that court case I was examined under oath so vigorously and relentlessly by the other lawyer that I decided to just quit the case, give the other side what they wanted, and not fight in court anymore."

My suspicions were all true—the fix was in. Everyone in the room was riveted as he filled in the details. I waited for the bombshell to drop, and tried to prepare myself for the shame, embarrassment, and ridicule that would surely follow. Strangely, even though I was expecting my ADR career to come to an end and my image to be shattered, I knew I would hold nothing against him. He was entitled to his feelings, and of course I had felt the same. In fact, I was grateful to him for helping me change my path in life, but of course he would never know that.

I focused on the consultant, feeling more uncomfortable by the minute as he continued telling his story. "That night I went to visit a very close friend," he said, "and told her how I'd broken down in court during the lawyer's cross examination. My friend asked me who this horrible lawyer was, and I told her it was Ernie Tannis." He pointed to me at the back of the room.

With the facts laid bare, I felt the shock, disbelief and disappointment in the room. It seemed as though every single person turned to stare at me, but all I could do was take a deep breath and shrug my shoulders. What else could I do? I desperately wanted to tell my side of the story—but who would believe me? It was too late.

"In a very strange coincidence," the consultant continued, "my friend said she also knew Ernie Tannis." This was a turn of events I had not been expecting, and I sat upright to listen. "She told me that Ernie had visited her earlier that evening, very upset and needing to talk. Ernie had not mentioned any names but had told her the story of the day in court. He described how horrible he felt about what had happened and wished there was some way he could apologize to the man he had cross examined so harshly.

> With the facts laid bare, I felt the shock, disbelief and disappointment.

"At that very moment," said the consultant, "I developed a great admiration for this lawyer who would have such feelings for a father in my situation, and who would show his humanity like that. I was grateful to have learned about this side of him."

The tension in the room was now loosening, and emotion was visible on several faces. It was hard for me to hold back the tears but I looked at him and managed to smile.

He continued: "So earlier this year when my colleague told me about the CICR and how Ernie was involved in trying to put something together in our country and our community, I decided I wanted to support what you are doing. I believe Ernie is true in his heart, and I wanted to have the chance to thank him."

I was flabbergasted—all these up-and-down emotions! I rose from my seat at the back of the room, he moved toward me, and when we met we shook hands then embraced.

"Thank you," I whispered.

"And thank you, too," he replied. It was one of those moments of gratitude and humility that lights up the dark.

Soon afterwards he invited me to his house and I met his daughter, who by then had grown into a lovely young woman. They showed me pictures of the times they had spent together after the divorce. He shared his story with her, and I was able to apologize to both of them face to face. What a gift. The three of us hugged with great affection.

It's not often we are able to come full circle like this, and to say I was enlightened would be an understatement. I learned so much about the interconnectedness of life.

## SOME LESSONS

- One never knows what effect, good or bad, your actions or words will have on someone else, but be aware that we all play a part in the lives of others, knowingly or unknowingly. This gentleman and I had a courtroom confrontation that ultimately had a deep and lasting effect on both our lives. Only because we shared our stories with the same friend were we able to learn, many years later, how very profound that effect had been. Usually we never know the impact that our words or conduct have on others.

- No matter how you try to avoid it, eventually everything catches up with you, and usually at unexpected moments. Know that and use it to prepare yourself to learn something new, or unlearn something from a previous event. As I learned through this experience, another person's story can help complete your own story, and the other way around.

- One of my favourite expressions is "It's not me that can't keep a secret, it's the people I tell!" There's often a deep fear of having our secrets exposed. Every person, every family, has deep, dark, secrets; indeed, whole cultures and nations harbour secret stories, or rewrite them to suit their purposes. In this story the gentleman and I each had a secret, but when he shared his secret story, I could then share mine, and it became one story that was no longer a secret. When the secrets are out, there's a reality check with what's going on. An earlier chapter in this book poses the question, "Is your house in order?" which to me has always meant the personal house of body, mind and spirit. My personal house was in disorder because of the secret I was keeping, but this man's story helped bring my house in order. From the Mohawk people at Akwesasne I learned the value of self-divulging, or sharing our stories with each other. We are all connected, and everyone has a story that could help someone else.

An earlier chapter discussed how a list should never be closed, and for me, the lessons in this book are never closed either. It is always inspiring and enlightening to hear the stories of others, and we are all better off for it. In many mediations I've seen that when people actively listen to each other and learn about others' stories, the dispute can be transformed from diatribe to dialogue, and we end up with ADR—A Dignified Resolution.

What is your story? I encourage you to share it and allow it to touch another. You never know the effect it might have. Thank you for allowing me to share mine.